More Tales From the Yankee Dugout

By
Ed Randall

Sports Publishing LLC
www.sportspublishingllc.com

Director of production: Susan M. Moyer
Dust jacket design: Joseph Brumleve
Interior art: Burke LaMotte

ISBN:1-58261-493-8

Printed in the United States of America

Sports Publishing LLC
www.sportspublishingllc.com

Dedication

To Big Ed and Nora for thinking me up and to Gracie, a living, breathing miracle, for her jaw-dropping, heart-stopping beauty, elegance, wit, grace, modesty, kindness, adorability, unwavering support and unconditional love.

This book is written in memory of those from September 11 whose spirit shines in the darkness and which most dramatically ratified our strength as a people.

The author shares with the world his grief at the loss of so many innocent lives, our pride in the courage and goodness of all those assisting the victims and our faith in the triumph of civilized behavior among all peoples.

Among those, Father Mychal Judge, who I will miss forever, for his wisdom and counsel that completely changed my attitude about life and love and his unbelievable ability to listen and fill those he listened to with their own dignity and to tell them that they were truly loved.

Acknowledgments

There is no bibliography in this book.
We therefore acknowledge all those within for their time, graciousness and accessibility, for which I am deeply grateful.

—Ed Randall

Contents

"Ed Randall has given us another brilliant collage of tales heroic and hilarious, major and minor that illuminate the Yankee saga. For this unforgiving Brooklyn Dodger fan, the worst has happened: the Yankees have become human. No reader can ever look at that intimidating group of hardened professionals in the same way again."

All the best, Pete Hamill

1
STARTING PITCHERS

Doug Drabek

What a start!

Doug Drabek, a pitcher Yankee fans still lament from a time the ballclub would habitually eat their young, had quite a debut in pinstripes in 1986.

After starting 1-4 with a 7.29 ERA in eight games for AAA Columbus, hardly numbers worthy of a call-up, Drabek was nonetheless summoned to the big club.

His first start came against Baltimore for Manager Lou Piniella, but as Drabek arrived at the ballpark, he had no idea he would get the ball.

"There were two balls in my locker. I said, 'Geez, you make it up here and they give you a brand-new ball.'"

Drabek pitched into the fifth inning when he was removed *without having allowed a hit and only one baserunner, a walk.*

"The first guy in the fifth got on on an error and I walked the next guy," said Drabek. "I didn't think anything of being taken out because I thought they gave the guy a hit. After the game, somebody brought it to my attention.

That's the first I knew I hadn't given up a hit. But I was just happy to have a chance to start."

Drabek was 7-8 his rookie season for a second-place Yankee team that finished 90-72, 5 1/2 games behind Boston. He was then traded that November with reliever Brian Fisher and a minor leaguer (where have you gone, Logan Easley?) for pitchers Rick Rhoden, Cecilio Guante and Pat Clements. Four years later, Drabek won 22 games for Pittsburgh and was named the National League Cy Young Award winner.

David Wells

Now it Can Be Told

Before deciding to play for the Yankees again in 2002, David Wells wanted to clear the air with once and future Manager Joe Torre.

"There were reports in the media saying that Joe really didn't care to have me back in New York," related Wells. "When I spoke with Joe, he said there was nothing to it."

Wells said if Joe didn't want him, why would he want to come back and play in New York for him? "It would just make things miserable."

Wells said he had a good conversation. "Joe said, 'The only reason why we traded you, it was Roger Clemens.' I understand that. Roger is a great pitcher."

David Wells

"It's just something that happened. It was a business transaction. I could never understand why they would trade someone who wanted to be here and spent the rest of their life as a Yankee and all of a sudden, it's gone," said Wells.

"The only thing you could come up with is Roger Clemens and I can understand it. So Joe and I hashed it out and it was great."

The Shirt off his Back and Back On It

Number 33 is back on the back of David Wells in a negotiation to be paid off later.

Yankees clubhouse manager Rob Cucuzza contacted last year's #33, Alfonso Soriano, upon the return of the Boomer. He gladly surrendered the uniform, never thinking to hold it hostage, though Wells offered a Rolex watch for its return.

"He had no problem giving up the number," said Wells. "That was a nice thing for him to do and I appreciate that."

Then Wells added, "It looks better on me. I have a wider back."

What Being a Yankee Means to Me

David Wells was always a rebel.

"I rooted for the Yankees as a kid because of the tradition. Everybody hated the Yankees when I was growing up. If someone hated something, I liked it," said Wells.

Wells remembers his Yankee introduction the first time.

"I walked right out to centerfield," remembered Wells, "and I got goosebumps like you wouldn't believe. Just having a dream come true playing in pinstripes was probably the best thing that every happened to me."

Now he is grateful for a return engineered solely by the Yankee owner.

"Most of all I want to thank George Steinbrenner very much for bringing me back." said Wells. "I think that was probably the best decision he's ever made and I thank him from the bottom of my heart."

Never In His Wildest Dreams

David Wells thought he would wear the Yankee pinstripes one day again.

"Yeah, as an Old Timer. You know how George likes to bring everybody back when you're 40, 50 years old and some," said Wells. "Coming back was never in my wildest dreams."

While on sabbatical from the Bronx, Wells had to get reaccustomed to going home after the regular season.

"In Toronto, the season would end around October 1 and I'd go up to my ranch in Michigan." It's the ranch he co-owns with former Tiger Kirk Gibson.

Wells got desperate.

"I'd go scouting around town looking for a Little League playoff game, to be honest with you," admitted Wells. "I was jonesing for a big game to pitch, even if it was with 10-year-olds. I'd blow it right by them."

Wells on Wells

"It was tough the last three years not being in the playoffs. That's something that I really strive for and look forward to.

"I'm not afraid to take that ball. I want to be the hero, I want to be the goat, it doesn't matter to me because I can still sleep at night knowing that I went out there and did my best.

"That's what you really play for, to get to the playoffs and eventually to the World Series.

"There's a lot of guys that get tight booties. I'm not the guy who gets that. I want the ball because I want to set the tone. You can't take the competitiveness out of me."

Dave LaPoint

Who Exactly is the Home Team?

Dave LaPoint was on the mound in Yankee Stadium at the moment it was announced that George Steinbrenner was banished from baseball by Commissioner Fay Vincent.

"We were playing Detroit. You know that everybody in the Stadium has their radio on. At that time, they all hated George and couldn't wait to hear something bad about him. I gave up a two-run home run to Cecil Fielder going the opposite direction and as the ball goes over the fence, the crowd let out with this tremendous roar."

LaPoint gave up his share of home runs, but never once did he experience a post-homer reaction like this.

"They're all celebrating. From the mound, it looks like they're gonna charge the field. Everybody's running down the aisles to get to the front row. It was at that very moment that they announced that George had been suspended and all the fans were cheering."

LaPoint said it was a terrible feeling.

"I don't know how many people were there that night but it was bad being on the mound. The reaction just towards one guy was unbelievable. At that time, you just felt bad for George. There they were in his house and they're acting like that."

Dock Ellis

A Throw-In

When the Yankees set their sights on the Pittsburgh Pirates as a trading partner in the winter of 1975, the object of their affection was a Triple-A second baseman from Brooklyn by the name of Willie Randolph.

"They wouldn't trade Willie unless the Yankees took me. The Pirates had to get me out of there. I had worn out my welcome. Danny Murtaugh and I didn't see eye to eye on certain things. The General Manager for the Pirates, Joe Brown, made a bet with the Yankees General Manager, that I would win more than 12 games."

Joe Brown was right. Dock Ellis won 17 games and one more in the playoffs.

Rabbit Ears

"One game that stands out from that 1976 season was a start I had in Milwaukee. I pitched against Bill Travers and lost like 1-0 or 2-0. But the thing I remember about it was these three little old ladies who sat behind home plate and they were calling my pitchers."

Ellis said they were there for every game, rain or shine. He estimated they were at least in their 60s.

"They would give little signs. Sometimes they would scream out, 'Throw that fastball, Dock, throw that fastball.' Or 'Throw that sinker, throw that sinker. He can't hit the sinker, throw it to him.' Or they would say, 'It's time for the pitch, it's time for the pitch.' In that particular game, I don't know if the wind was blowing right or whatever but I could hear their every whim. I used to be rabbit eyes when I was younger but after that, I couldn't hear anything. But those ladies I could hear."

The Circus is in Town

For Dock Ellis, there was nothing like playing for the New York Yankees.

"It really didn't dawn on me until years later what guys dreamed to do. And that was to play for the Yankees. I don't what it is. It was totally different. I had been with the Pirates and we would come in and kick butt every day with The Lumber Company and stuff. But with the Yankees, you were on exhibit. It was like people just came to look at you. They were in awe of you."

As Dock says, "You had to do what you had to do.

"You had to sign all the autographs, you had to talk baseball to the people and if you're in New York, you had to make sure to ask them if they were a Yankee fan or a Met fan. Or are you just over here to watch us and you're a Met fan?"

Bobby Brown

Dr. Bobby Brown, Noted Cardiologist, That Story is True

The idea that Bobby Brown would be a roommate of Yogi Berra's is a perfectly reasonable notion. The idea that one would be reading medical books while the other was reading comic books sounds apocryphal.

"I had to take some exams when I got back to school following the 1946 season, my rookie year. I had to take pathology and pharmacology exams. I had completed the courses except for two weeks and they were long courses. They took almost three-fourths of our school year so they were big exams. I took my pathology book on the road and would I would study it during the day when we weren't playing."

His roommate was not studying pathology.

"Yogi would read comic books. They were 10 cents apiece in those days. He'd buy a dollar's worth. One night, we both finished about the same time. I closed my book and he closed his comic book, looked at me and said, "So how did yours come out?"

Lucky 7

In 41 postseason at-bats, Bobby Brown had an astounding .707 slugging percentage.

"I had 18 hits and nine of them for extra-bases."

It's as if playing in the Series was nothing special.

"It was just one of those things were things happened to work out. I can't tell you why. I always thought it was because I was hidden in that line-up. We had so damn many good hitters that they breathed a sigh of relief when they saw me coming up."

Brown used to hit sixth. In one Series against Brooklyn, he hit fifth.

"I was hitting behind Yogi and DiMaggio and those guys. I sneaked by and didn't embarrass myself anyway."

Yogi

Bobby Brown first met Yogi as minor leaguers with the Yankees' Newark farm club, a team that, at first, did not take him seriously.

"I guess about 10 days after the season started, we were in Rochester on our first road-trip. We heard that we were gonna get a pitcher named Monk Dubiel who was coming down from the Yankees. He reported and along with him was this little guy and no one knew who he was. Dubiel said the Yankees had told him to bring him along.

"I said, 'What's his name?' He said, 'His name is Yogi.'

"He didn't even know his last name.

"Nobody could believe he was a player. When he came into the clubhouse, the trainer looked at him and wouldn't give him a locker. He said, 'Just hang your clothes on the nail over there.' Yogi said, 'I'm a player. I have a contract to play with this team.'"

The manager was no refuge either.

"George Selkirk was the manager and he looked at him. You know how he looked in a uniform. So Selkirk says, 'Listen, we only get 30 minutes to hit on the road. I don't want you to take up the time of the regulars hitting. You just kind of shag balls in the outfield till we get to Newark and then we'll work you out.' They wouldn't even let him hit."

The first day of the homestand in Newark, Selkirk had Yogi at the park for his 2 p.m. audition.

"We had a night game that night and I went out there at five o'clock.

"Selkirk was sitting there in the clubhouse kind of staring off into space. I said, 'George, how did Yogi do?' He said, 'He hit them over the light towers.' That's when he started playing and never sat down again."

Looks can be deceiving.

Ralph Branca

Who Knew?

Ralph Branca, the personification of the Brooklyn Dodgers, moved on Detroit where he pitched with a bad hose. That would explain his release during the '54 season, returning to his native Mt. Vernon and taking matters into his own hands.

"The Tigers' general manager was one of those know-it-alls who never talked to the trainer. After I got released, I came home and started throwing at the local field. The Yankees, at the time, were on the road. When they got home, I picked up the phone and called Casey and asked if I could work out. I thought I still could pitch.

"I'm warming up on the sideline near home plate to throw batting practice and Jim Turner, the pitching coach, looks at me and he said, 'Hey, you didn't throw like that at Detroit.' I said, 'No, I was pitching with a sore arm.' That was always one of my faults, I always wanted the ball. Other guys had sore arms and they didn't pitch but I kept pitching. It ended up that the Yankees signed me."

Ralph said it wasn't weird donning pinstripes.

"I played against the Yankees and knew many of them. I was friendly with Whitey and Yogi, knew Mickey, and Lopat became a good friend. I really wasn't a total stranger."

So why did he pick up the phone and call the Yankees and not the Dodgers?

"Well, I guess they were home."

Branca didn't pitch a whole lot for a Yankee club that won 103 games and went home, losing out to the 111-win Cleveland Indians.

"I started in Baltimore and threw a knee-high pitch and the umpire wouldn't give it to me and I wasn't smart enough to raise my sights two inches. The strike zone in the National League was the knee and in the American League from the top of the knee and this guy called it that way. The National League was a low-ball league and the American

League was a high-ball league. I can remember Rizzuto yelling at the ump from shortstop, 'Where are those pitches?'

"I probably walked about four or five guys and only pitched about four innings. But they only got one run off me.

"Then my next start was on Old Timers Day against the Red Sox and I went seven innings. The score was 1 to 1 and Moose Skowron got a basehit with men on pinch-hitting for me and the Yankees won the game and I won the game 3 to 1."

But disappointment was warming up in the bullpen.

"The next week I went up to Boston and figured I would pitch again. I had only given up three or four hits but I didn't pitch. They put me in the bullpen. I gave up a run, but the Yankees got a couple of runs. I would have been the winning pitcher but whoever came in didn't hold the lead. And I don't think I pitched after that."

Ralph Branca had a bonus coming if he stayed with them. They didn't want to pay that bonus so they released him after the season. He then signed with the New York Giants' top farm club in Minneapolis.

"Some people still come up to me and remember me with the Yankees. They saw my picture somewhere in a Yankee uniform. Number 24."

Bill Monboquette

Don't Shut the Door

Bill Monboquette was the only reliable starter for a series of horrible Boston clubs throughout the early 60s. The rotation was Bill Monboquette and then wait four days. After being dealt to Detroit, he was released and then signed with the Yankees in 1967.

"We had a rookie on our club by the name of Charlie Sands. Mantle, I guess, got talking with Ralph Houk, and said, 'We'll set him up.'"

There was one rule about paying a visit to The Major's office.

"If you had to go in, you don't shut the door. Mantle went over to Charlie and said, 'Ralph wants to see you.' And of course, Charlie didn't know what to think. 'What does he want to see me for?'"

Mantle told Sands, "When you go in there, make sure you don't shut the door." Apparently, once upon a time, somebody did shut the door and Houk got ticked at him. A reputation was born.

"So Charlie went in and Ralph said, 'Shut the door.' And Sands said, 'No way, I'm not shutting the door.' Again, Ralph says, 'Shut the door.' And Sands says, 'I can't shut the door.' Ralph then threatened him, 'If you don't shut the door . . . .'"

"I guess it was so funny that Ralph couldn't hold it back and he started to laugh. Mantle was going absolutely bananas. He loved to do things like that. I was dying laughing myself."

Playing With the Hall of Fame

Bill Monboquette's career spanned a living, breathing Hall of Fame.

"I had the privilege of playing three years with Ted Williams, five with Yastrzemski, a little more than a year and a half with Kaline in Detroit, and then I played with Mantle and Ford. Then I got traded to San Francisco for Lindy McDaniel and I got a chance to play with Mays, McCovey, Marichal and Perry."

All of which fell on deaf ears one day.

"I told the kids this one time when I was coaching for the Bluejays in St. Catherine's. A couple of guys said to me, 'Well, who are they?' and now I was really mad then. I said, 'Well, I'll tell you what. They're all Hall of Famers and they never acted like you kids do.' I think they got the message right there. The respect for the game, I don't know if it's there like it used to be. It's a shame because it's an awful great game."

Sam McDowell

Pitching on Fumes

In 1973, the Yankees acquired Sam McDowell from San Francisco, who had traded away future Hall of Famer Gaylord Perry, to get him.

"Being an alcoholic, I met the team in Oakland and showed up drunk from the night before. Fortunately, I sobered up. I did fairly well for a while because I was kind of a semi-controlled drunk. When I say 'semi-controlled', most of most career I was a control drunk in which I never drank the night before or the day that I was pitching thinking somehow that would help me. Most of it was superstition and had nothing to do with drinking because, of course, I never knew I had a problem. The denial was so strong in me as it is in, I guess, everybody.

"Then my arm in the middle of the season started to hurt. That was when my drinking just kept escalating."

Helping Others to Help Themselves

Recovery. That is the theme of Sam McDowell's post-baseball-playing life, his and others.

"What was sad was after I was thrown out of baseball by the Pittsburgh Pirates and eventually went through my own recovery, I still didn't believe that I had the right to help anybody else. I was just so frightened and scared of hurting somebody by giving them any advice. I just kind of stayed to myself."

Eventually, McDowell went to Pitt for course work to understand the intricacies of drug and alcohol addiction and to understand different types of therapies.

"I became a therapist and figured that since I burned too many bridges in baseball and would never be asked back, I went ahead and started my own practice with teenagers trying to help them with their difficulties and problems."

For 18 years, Sam McDowell was the therapist for the Texas Rangers in sports psychology, addictions and prevention programs. He has also been a consulting therapist for the Baseball Assistance Team for the past 14 years.

Bob Tewksbury

Been There, Done That

Here's a question for you, Bob.

Now that you're coaching Little League, is there anything you take from your days as a major leaguer and impart to the kids?

"Tom Kelly has a great phrase: to play the game. I remember when Mike Pagliarulo who was a teammate on the Yankees was on the World Series team with the Twins in '91. When I played with him in Texas in '95, that was his saying."

That was what the Twins have always done.

"They've always played the game. They have always been noticed for the way they hustle to first, the way they carry themselves on and off the field, the way they do these things and it's not coincidental."

Tewksbury imparts that lesson.

"What I try to say to these kids is we're gonna go out and we're gonna play the game. I don't care if we're gonna play the first-place team or the last-place team, I don't care what line-up I'm sending out there, if it's the best little leaguer or the not-so-talented little leaguer, but we're just to play the game and have fun."

Tommy John

Having seen the other side, Tewksbury enjoys his work but doesn't take it too seriously.

"I laugh at all the people who think that their kid is gonna be the next Ken Griffey Jr. and they have batting gloves and baseball camps year-round.

"And they're 10."

Tommy John

On Tommy John Surgery

Tommy John hasn't pitched since 1989 and yet, he sees his name in the paper with alarming regularity. And it alarms him.

"Never in my wildest dreams did I think that it was going to happen all these times when I had it done back in '74. I just thought I was the unlucky guy who had a misfortune. The problem that I see is why are all these guys having it?"

John thinks the fault lies with everyone in baseball, from the coaches in high school and college and strength coaches.

"Dr. Andrews has done over 1,000 now. Dr. Jobe has done well over 1,000 and there are probably two or three thousand other doctors out there that are doing the same surgery numerous times. So we have to be doing something wrong as to why these kids are having it. Dr. Andrews just operated on a kid 15 years old. He said that should never, ever, ever, ever happen."

John's personal feeling is these kids have been sold a bill of goods that they can become better pitchers if they go in the weight room and begin lifting.

"You become a better pitcher by pitching, by throwing the ball. And I think, personally, we've got to get back to think things the way they used to be done. I realize the methods and the training are much better. But something's wrong when all these guys are having Tommy John surgery.

"It's nice to see your name out there and you know that the surgery is bringing guys off the scrap heap but there's a reason why they're having to have the surgery and I think something is wrong in the training programs."

9/11

Through sheer coincidence, Tommy John literally had a bird's eye view of the tragedy at the World Trade Center.

"I was landing at LaGuardia Airport. We were on final approach. The pilot informed us that both towers were on fire. In fact, my wife's got a picture of the World Trade Center burning from the window of the airplane as we were making a right-hand turn going up the East River."

Nobody on board knew what had happened.

"I thought there was a grease fire or something in the restaurant of one of the buildings. And then when we saw the smoke billowing, I thought there had been a gas explosion or something. We had a friend of ours who worked down there on Wall Street and we couldn't get through on the phone. Then, we called his wife and she told us what happened. My wife told others about the turn of events and cellphones started coming out all over the place."

Stan Bahnsen

When Baseball Was Baseball

Once upon a time, pitchers were required to bat in the American League.

When Stan Bahnsen pitched for the Yankees, he was joined in the starting rotation by Mel Stottlemyre, Fritz Peterson and Mike Kekich.

"We had a contest where it was Fritz and I against Mel and Kekich to see which team would get the most hits in a season. This was about 1970. We would have a cutoff date near the end of the season. Wherever we were at the time, the two winners were entertained by the two losers to the finest restaurant in town. It was carte blanche, you could order whatever you wanted, any food, any champagne, anything."

The cutoff date coincided with the Yankees in Cleveland.

"You not only got points for hits, you got a point for hitting a batter.

"Kekich and Stottlemyre edged Fritz and I by a couple of points. They wanted to go to a place called The Kon Tiki which was a Polynesian place that I think was located in the

Stan Bahnsen

Sheraton. They had all the fancy mai tais and all the exotic drinks and appetizers."

At the same time they were eating and drinking like kings, the winners were being royally screwed.

"We had to foot the bill but what Stottlemyre didn't know was that we had his American Express card. We got it out of where they keep the valuables in the clubhouse and returned it the next day. They were ordering food they weren't even gonna eat. They've got mai tais, the appetizers, all these drinks with umbrellas in them, extra egg rolls. We're like, 'That's fine, that's fine. You guys won.' They were trying to get our goat. What they didn't know was Stottlemyre was paying for this whole thing. Fritz and I staged this argument when the bill came, 'I'll get it, no, I'll get it.'"

After the season, the United States Postal Service delivered the latest American Express bill to the Stottlemyre residence.

"I remember that about a month after the season, Fritz and I got phone calls from Mel. He was really hot. His wife saw the bill and she says, 'What was this?'"

They did end up paying Stottlemyre back.

"He never missed the card because he wasn't paying for anything that night. But he did pay for everything that night."

Is That Who I Think It Is?

Fritz Peterson developed a reputation as an instigator of practical jokes. But this was Stan Bahnsen at his best.

"Mike Kekich had bought a waterbed. They had just come out in the late 60s, early 70s. We are on a nine- or 10-day road trip and he had bought one in Chicago. It was in a box that was about 20 inches square. I asked him what was in the box. He said, 'I just got a waterbed.' I said, 'We'll probably use an ice pick to punch some holes in it before the roadtrip is over.'"

Soon, the waterbed was nowhere to be found.

"Nobody could figure out where it was. I don't know how he hid it. We figured he must have shipped it back because he was worried about sabotage."

The last game of the long road trip was in Milwaukee.

"I come into the clubhouse and my locker was by Kekich's. I saw a box under some towels and it was the damn waterbed. I wasn't gonna poke holes in it, but I wanted to play a trick on him."

Let the chicanery begin.

"At County Stadium, the top of the scoreboard had an automobile on top of it. If anybody hit for the cycle, they win this car. It's up there on a platform. It must have been lifted up there with a crane. I gave the clubhouse kid 10 bucks and told him I wanted him to drape this waterbed over the top of the car. And he did it."

Batting practice is over and the pitchers are running together in the outfield.

"I made it a point to be by Kekich because I wanted to get him to look at the scoreboard because he never would. Every time we would run a sprint, I would look back. Finally, he says, 'What do you keep looking at?' I said, 'I'm just trying to check the out-of-town scores.' After a while, he says, 'What game are you looking at?' I said, 'The Baltimore game.' That was at the top of the scoreboard.

And then Mike Kekich turned around and saw his waterbed.

"This was about 20-30 minutes before game time. He sees this black thing draped over this compact car. He went crazy. He quit running with me and went into the clubhouse to get his game uniform on. Then I saw him running out toward center field."

To get to the platform atop the scoreboard, there was a catwalk that was straight up about 75 feet, a very intimidating presence.

"He went all the way up this ladder to this trap door. But there was a lock on it. He had to come all the way back down the ladder and had to go find someone who had a key for this lock. He finally found someone who had the key."

The timing couldn't have been any better.

"They just started to play the national anthem. The flagpole is right next to the scoreboard. They're playing, 'Oh say, can you see' and this trap door opens and here comes Kekich up on top of the scoreboard in his #18 Yankee uniform and he's pulling his waterbed off the top of that car. It was so funny."

Kekich accused Bahnsen of planting the waterbed on the scoreboard. Bahnsen vigorously denied it. As payback, before the flight back to New York, Kekich got hold of some luggage tags and placed them on Bahnsen's bags.

They read "Honolulu."

That's A Lock

The Yankees had just lost a doubleheader in Chicago on getaway day.

"Fritz got into this lock thing. He would get bicycle padlocks and lock stuff up. I had these shoes with buckles on them and Fritz locked them together. I had to be on the bus in five minutes. I'm sitting in my locker and I'm so mad. I know who did it. I'm like screw it, I'm not going to LA."

As the manager, Ralph Houk is the last guy to leave for the bus. He sees Bahnsen and asks the obvious question.

"He says, 'Bahnsen, what's goin' on?' I say, 'I can't go.' He says, 'Why can't you go?' I say, 'I can't put my shoes on.' He was not in a very good mood. He says, 'Why can't you?' I say, 'Because they're locked together.' He says, 'Well, somebody better get you a goddamn key because if you don't make that bus, you're gonna get fined.' Somehow they got a key and I made the bus by about a minute."

Jim Bouton

Hats Off

Because baseball is all about statistical overload, somebody actually counted the number of times Jim Bouton's hat flew off his head during his World Series victory over the Cardinals in Game Three of the 1964 World Series.

The answer is 47.

"The hat came off because of my pitching motion. I used the trunk of my body to get a lot of my velocity. This means that the top part of my body would propel forward so I would use my legs, my arm and the forward motion of my body and I used the top part of my body more than most pitchers. Because of that snapping action, my hat would pop off my head. I had problems with that in the minors. It was nothing that just started happening at Yankee Stadium."

This started when Bouton started throwing the ball hard.

"Toward the end of my last year in the minor leagues, my 1961 season when I was pitching in the Texas League for Amarillo, my hat would start coming off my head. That's when my velocity got up pretty high."

Bouton doesn't know how hard he was throwing because they didn't have radar guns in those days.

"I would estimate it probably somewhere about 105 to 110 miles an hour."

A Fish Story A.K.A. It Sounds Fishy to Me

During spring training in 1963, on the morning after a night game, it was time for Mickey Mantle's fishing contest in the canals of Fort Lauderdale.

"You would go there with your roommate, leave the dock at 8 a.m. and come back at noon. Everybody would put 20 bucks or something like that and at the end, the boat that caught the most fish would spilt the pot with the boat that caught the biggest fish."

Bouton says that he and his roommate, the legendary Phil Linz, were terrible fishermen.

"Linz and I are driving along this highway in Florida about seven o'clock in the morning and we see a bait & tackle store along the side of the road. There was a freezer out in front of the place."

Bouton told Linz to pull in. He had a hunch.

"I was gonna buy a fish, but the place was closed. But I happened to open the freezer and there was this gigantic fish inside, probably something from the sea. It was huge, probably about 25 pounds, a monster fish. It might have

Jim Bouton

been a bass or tuna. I see this guy and I say, 'How much do you want for this fish?' He says, 'Oh, you can have it. That's been in there for three years. You can't eat it.' I say, 'That's OK, we don't need to eat it.'

Bouton and Linz left with the fish and put it in the bottom of the cooler that had beer and sandwiches in it and covered it with ice.

"We get out to our boat, get out around the corner, took the fish out of the cooler, attached a line to it and dunked him in the water. Our only hope was that he would thaw out by the time we came back to the dock. It was frozen stiff, solid as a rock. Everyone once in a while, we would lift him out of the water and put a little sun on him to see how he was thawing out."

Now they're playing pretend.

"We're out there fishing and of course, we're not catching a damn thing."

They don't have to. They have the thing won.

"We know we have the winner. We know we have the biggest fish and we may even also win for poundage. We know we're in pretty good shape."

That's when Tom Tresh and Joe Pepitone drove by.

"Hey, how you guys doing?" We say, 'We caught a couple.' They say, 'Let's see what you got.' We said, 'Well, we're only gonna show you part of it.' We lifted it about a third of the way up and they said some bad words."

Bouton and Linz made sure they were the last ones back to the dock so that they could make a grand entrance.

"We pull up to the dock and there the players are with fish all spread out. Whitey and Mickey have about 15 fish, Boyer and Stafford have about eight fish of decent size, a couple of nice five- or six-pounders in there."

And now it is showtime.

"We haul our fish off the boat and lay him down next to all these other fish. It looked like our guy could have eaten all the rest of them for lunch and have plenty of room left over. They weighed it and it was something like 22 pounds."

Bouton and Linz were awarded half the money for cheating. But that's not the end of the story.

"Sometime later, Mickey came over to me and said, 'I've been thinking about that fish. How come ours were green and flipping around and yours was gray and just lying there?' I said, 'We caught him first thing in the morning and we were dragging him around all day.'"

Ryne Duren

That'll Show 'Em

Ryne Duren can't remember the exact first time it happened but he does recall 1958 as being the year in which he began firing his first warm-up pitch onto the screen behind home plate.

"That's the season Bob Turley had the great year. For some reason or another, he didn't like much drop in the mound. He liked it a little flat, maybe because he kind of came from the side. He went to the groundcrew and asked them if they could make less slope in front of the rubber."

Duren was warming up in the bullpen where that mound had a very different feel.

"You released the ball in coordination with when your foot came down. What I did was kind of like the artillery: you fired the first one and then zeroed in from there. I came in and threw that first ball real hard. I thought my knee was gonna hit my chest. But my foot got down so fast I had to release the ball or I'd tear myself apart. The foot triggers the release. So that ball went way up on the screen. That's how it happened the first time."

Casey Stengel, Frank Crosetti and the press corps thought it was great.

Did he do it in every game?

"Absolutely not. I would do it every once in a while for the hell of it. This was after I was well established. I sure wouldn't want to do it as a rookie. Nobody likes a smart-ass rookie, you know how that goes.

"Crosetti always thought it was great. He always thought it intimidated the opposition. I never felt so."

A Most Unlikely Scenario

During the 1961 season, the Yankees traded Ryne Duren to the expansion Los Angeles Angels for pitcher Tex Clevinger and to reacquire outfielder Bob Cerv. Later on that season, Duren was taken out of the bullpen to start against Turley.

"Bill Rigney thought, 'Maybe Duren's got something to prove.' In the sixth inning, they were beating me one to nothing. Mantle had a grounder and I had to cover first. He carried me across first base and down the right field line so as not to run over me. Kubek scored from second base."

In the bottom of the sixth inning, the Angels had the bases loaded and Duren was the due hitter.

"If there was one out, Rigney would have had to pinch-hit for me. But since I was pitching well, he let me hit. Turley got two quick strikes on me and he kind of nodded as if trying to get me thinking."

Duren says you never pitch a guy with glasses up in his eyes. Turley did.

"He threw another fastball, this one out of the strike zone and a little bit high. I hit that choked-up-bat grounder right past him and Kubek and Richardson both just about got it before it rolled into centerfield for a single. Two to one. Then little Albie Pearson came up behind me and hit the first pitch out of the ballpark into the short right field bleachers in the old LA park. People in the stands went crazy from the time I hit that ball until the ballgame was over. I think I was relieved in the eighth inning and got the win."

When Bill Rigney died last year, his daughter called Duren and told him that of all of the things that happened while he was in baseball, he talked about that the most.

Mike Torrez

A Chili Reception

This is how Mike Torrez came from Oakland to the Yankees.

"Charlie loved making chili. He was in the clubhouse and he had made some chili. He made pretty good chili. We were talking about him giving me the recipe. He wanted to sign me for a three-year contract at that time for $75,000, $125,000 and $150,000."

That's all beneath today's major league minimum salary.

"I said, 'Thanks for the three years but that's not enough money. You gotta come up with more money, that's nothing.' He said, 'Mike, if I can't sign you, I'm gonna try to trade you.' I said, 'That's fine.'"

Now the As are in Anaheim and Torrez is in the hotel lobby reading the paper. Joe Romo, the trainer at the time comes over and says he has a phone call. It's Charlie.

"I go over to the phone and he says, 'Doggone it, Mike, I'd love to keep you but it doesn't like I'm gonna be able to, so I made a deal. I traded you to the Yankees for some players.' I said, 'Well, alright' and went over to the stadium to get my stuff out of the locker. That's how the deal was made."

A Different Perspective on B. Dent's Fly Ball

Here's the question: if Bucky Dent does not foul the ball off his foot and there's a stoppage in play, is history different?

"Probably. I was in a good groove. I was concentrating well. I had to get restarted again and on that first pitch, it was like 'goddamn it.'"

And then Torrez watched.

"Up until that point, the balls were not going anywhere. There was a little wind blowing in. For some reason, later in the afternoon, about the sixth inning, it changed and started blowing out. I was walking off the mound toward the dugout and looking up thinking I was out of the inning. I saw Yaz and thought that he had it. He looks up and sonofabitch…"

Mel Stottlemyre

Mr. Grand Slam Himself

In 1965, Mel Stottlemyre won 20 games for a Yankee club that only won 77, pitched 18 complete games and led the league with 291 innings pitched. Oh, and hit a grand slam . . . inside the park.

"We were in New York playing Boston. I think it was in about the fifth inning. We were behind in the game and the pitcher was Bill Monboquette. I think the pitch was a hanging slider on the outside part of the plate. With me being a pitcher, Yastrzemski was playing shallow in left. The centerfielder was shading me toward right so there was this huge gap in left-center."

Stottlemyre hit a line-drive.

"It was just like a line-drive single but it was hit right in that gap and rolled forever out there in left-centerfield. I knew right away that it was extra bases, but I remember coming around third and was completely shocked when Frank Crosetti kept waving his arms in the coach's box for me to go on. It was such a long distance between third and home and everybody thought I made a great slide at home. To be honest with you, it was a fall."

Stottlemyre won the game 6-3.

Who Wants to Pitch?

The 1969 All-Star Game in Washington, D.C. was scheduled to be the first one ever played at night. Problem was it poured and was played the next afternoon. Either time, Denny McLain was tabbed to start for the American League.

Paging Mr. Denny McLain. Mr. Denny McLain to the white courtesy telephone.

"It was a shocker to me that I was going to start. I didn't know until I got to the ballpark. I'm on the bus and knew I had a good chance to get an inning or two in. I didn't know up until about 45 minutes before the game that I was starting. Denny McLain just never showed up. It was a thrill even though I lost the game. I would have preferred my start was under some other circumstances at least knowing about it and that sort of thing."

Mel Stottlemyre hung a slider to Johnny Bench for a two-run homer and was the losing pitcher as the American League was defeated 9-3. Nobody ever did find Denny McLain.

A Cancer Survivor's Survivor

Since 2000, Mel Stottlemyre has defined courage in his fight against a cancer that knows no cure, multiple myeloma. This, after losing an 11-year-old son to leukemia.

"Myeloma was found through a regular team physical. I didn't know what myeloma was and how serious it was. I found out it was a disease of the blood. I was real concerned and I guess was a little bit scared. But the more I found out about the disease and the more reassuring things I got from my doctor helped tremendously. I think my attitude changed after I went to see the doctor at Sloan-Kettering. He painted a much different picture than what I had been told by the doctors previously in Florida. It was a tremendous shock. My disease, fortunately, was smoldering and I went 13 months before I had to start treatment. I think in a sense this probably was a little blessing for me. I knew I was gonna have to face the treatment but I had an opportunity to think about it ahead of time. I think my attitude changed a great deal. I became more optimistic about the treatments that were available through my doctor in New York at Sloan-Kettering."

In at least one other cancer survivor's eyes, Mel Stottlemyre has become a living, breathing testimony to those people who think that diagnosis is a death sentence.

"It isn't. I think we've come so far in recent years with the treatments and the things they can do for the disease. We can't talk about a cure but they are very optimistic about extending our lives. Naturally, I don't feel good about having the disease. But I feel real good that things have gone very positively for me and I've been able to paint a different picture than what we had before, that the word 'cancer' when it strikes us, everything has to completely change in our life. I don't think it does. Through the modern-day care that we have where things have gotten better, I think if we so chose we can continue the normal life we had before. Still in the back of our mind that word is always there and we have to learn to live with it. But it certainly isn't as drastic as it was as recently as just five or ten years back."

Perspective

One former cancer patient sees losses differently.

"I don't think I take the losses any lighter. I've always hated to lose or to accept losing unless you lose the right way. I feel real bad when one of my guys has a bad day."

But the sting is less.

"It certainly doesn't last as long. I look at things and think, 'Well, it's a loss but it's gonna pass quickly. We've got tomorrow to try and make it up.' So my attitude toward those things has changed greatly. I joke with some of the guys sometimes when they're so perturbed about some little thing that may be happening in baseball or it may be a thing that's happening in their life that's a very simple thing. It's not anything that's life-threatening or anything like that. And I really downplay those things. I say, 'That's nothing.' It's not life or death. It really has made me look at my entire life and people around me in a much different way.'"

Me too.

Stottlemyre vs. Stottlemyre

The only element missing from the electric 2001 World Series would have been for Mel Stottlemyre to have the opportunity to watch his son, Todd, pitch for Arizona against his Yankees.

"That would have been a huge thrill. I felt bad when we lost. I thought it was a great Series. As great a Series as it was for the Arizona Diamondbacks, it still was kind of tainted, I think, in Todd's mind because of the fact that he wasn't able to perform."

It's something the two Stottlemyres had long talked about.

"We've come close. We've had playoff games, we've had regular-season games where he's been on the other side. I tell you what, I'm sure whether I'm really up for it. I think the Series itself would have been even more emotional."

Al Downing

The Only Game in Town

When Al Downing signed a professional contract with the Yankees in 1961, they were the only game in town.

"You have understand the times that were happening in baseball. The Dodgers had both gone to the West Coast in '58. Not only were the only team in New York, they were basically the kings of the major leagues. That's not to be facetious. They were a ballclub that epitomized baseball. And when you stop and think about it, a lot of the legislation that came about subsequently was aimed at the success of the Yankees such as the free-agent draft, expansion and stuff like that. You had the freedom to sign with whomever you wanted to when I did. You signed with the best ballclub. The best ballclub was the Yankees."

But there was more to it than that.

"The Giants had sent somebody to look at me, the Washington Senators did the same thing, the Pittsburgh Pirates and the Phillies. But there was a common attraction. The fellow who tried to sign me for the Phillies when I came out of high school signed me a year-and-a-half later for the Yankees. That's pretty much how I wound up with the Yankees. It wasn't as if they were knocking my door down. It was because of this one particular scout that I signed with the Yankees."

Guesswork

Al Downing held opponents to a league-low .184 average his first year in the majors in 1963 and led the league in strikeouts with 217 in his second. Hard to believe he didn't know what he was doing on the mound. Could've fooled us.

"In my own mind I was disappointed that I didn't have better success. As I look back in retrospect, someone once said that youth is wasted on the young. I felt that I didn't learn how to pitch until I had been in the major leagues about five years. I always use that as a yardstick because you basically don't know what you're doing. So you're pretty much pitching on anxiety and instinct, not knowledge because you don't have much knowledge. That's why I don't feel that I had great success because I felt that my better years were still ahead of me."

Then Al Downing hurt his arm in 1967.

2
RELIEF PITCHERS

Paul Gibson

Walk a Mile in My Shoes

Paul Gibson's story with the Yankees is not about relief pitching but his memories of "Wade Boggs and his crazy superstitions."

He says that Boggs was very superstitious about his spikes. When he got hits, he would wear the same shoes.

"One particular night, we had a rain delay. He's walking around and his shoes are soaking wet. Everyone else is changing their shoes, socks and everything and he won't take his shoes off."

Naturally, the team was getting on him a little bit.

"After the rain delay ends, he comes in and throws the shoes in the garbage and puts a new pair of shoes on. I took the shoes out of the garbage and put them in my locker thinking they would be used for an auction someday, get him to sign them."

That's what he thought.

"Two innings later, he came back in and asked the clubhouse guy where the shoes were because he had struck out again and he wanted the old shoes back. So he retrieved the shoes from my locker and made the clubhouse guy take the shoelaces out and put new shoelaces in. That was the problem."

Obviously.

Hey, Let's Have a Catch . . . Now!!

And then Wade Boggs wanted to have a catch.

"He used to play catch in front of the dugout. A specific number of throws. He would grab the same guy every time. When I was there, it was Charlie Wonsowicz, the batting practice pitcher. No matter where he was, he had to be there at 7:13. Boggs wouldn't leave the dugout until the clock the clock ticked :13. He would make 13 or 14 tosses and the last one he would throw a knuckleball. So that night, I told Charlie when he gets ready to throw the last one, walk off. 'Don't let him throw you the ball. Just walk off the field.' Freaked out, Boggs was totally freaked out."

Boggs was hardly alone with his superstitions.

"Paul O'Neill was very similar. There was a young player who had just come up who was living up in Westchester. He wanted a ride to the ballpark. O'Neill was on a real hot streak. He was driving to the park by himself. The only person who could give this guy a ride from Westchester to the ballpark was O'Neill."

O'Neill refused.

"I think he had hit three home runs in four days or something like that. He refused him a ride to the ballpark because of that."

Lunchtime! Now!

Don't eat with Wade Boggs. Paul Gibson found out the hard way.

"We were in Oakland and I had had lunch with Wade at a restaurant. He got four hits that day. The next day he calls me in the room and he says, 'We're gonna go eat again.' I said, 'Well, I don't feel like eating this early.' He says, 'No, you have to eat with me.' I said, 'OK, I'll go with you.' He says to the maitre'd at the restaurant, 'We want that table over there.'"

It gets better.

"We get the same table we had before. He made me sit in the same seat that I sat in the day before. He made me order the same lunch that I had the day before. That was the kind of thing you dealt with with those two guys."

Goose Gossage

Goose on Mo

"The first time that I saw him was in the Seattle play-offs in '95. I was watching it on TV at home in Colorado. He came into a bases-loaded situation and I looked at this kid get out of it without giving up a run. I'll tell you, right then I knew. I said, 'This kid is special'. But until he came up with the cutter, I think that he was starting to become hittable. Now, he has evolved into the game's best closer and has been just unhittable. That's not telling anybody any secrets. He has been flawless."

Then there is the emotional aspect of Rivera's appearance.

"There is nothing worse than being in the opposing dugout to watch a guy like that come into the ballgame and what a disheartening, sinking feeling it is."

He should know.

When I'm 64

Jesse Orosco, along with Terry Mulholland, whose performances may both date back to the first-ever boxscore in 1823, is reported to have told his wife he sees no reason why he cannot pitch in the major leagues until age 50. He receives support from Goose Gossage, who pitched until age 43.

"I'm 50 right now and I still throw batting practice to my son. My arm feels great. I don't see any reason why a relief pitcher being used correctly and sporadically in tough situations couldn't pitch until 50. The way the guys stay in shape today only helps their chances. Rick Honeycutt pitched until he was 43 or 44. If you're lefthanded, especially if you are lefthanded, you can come in and get one lefthander out. I don't put it beyond the realm that you could pitch until you're 50 years old."

John Habyan

The Steal Sign

Time for a tale from the bullpen.

"One that stands out is that the Yankee bullpen has always been accused of tipping our hitters with signs from the opposing team. We're giving location. This day, we're playing Texas in Yankee Stadium."

There would be a line of guys in the bullpen who would sit up close to the wall on a bench. Here's how it worked.

"We would have one guy in a blue top, usually a jacket. Remember Carl Taylor? He did it most of the time. Everybody would wear white, so he would stick out. All we'd do is if he ate a sunflower seed, that meant the catcher was setting up in. If he didn't do anything, he was setting up away. We did this for a few series and some of the guys were having some pretty good success with it.

"Not everybody took advantage of the locale signs, but a few of the hitters did it because if the guy set up in, he pretty much knew it was a fastball.

"So it's this one afternoon against the Rangers. I think it's the third game of the series and we had been doing a pretty good job against them. All of a sudden, this little bat boy comes out to the bullpen, a little kid."

He had a note and it wasn't from his teacher.

"We read the note and it was from Bobby Valentine. It said, 'If that guy eats one more seed, the next guy's gonna catch it right in the dome.'"

That's when they told Carl Taylor to quit eating and shut it down.

"That's pretty good that he picked it up, though.

Paging Mr. Redass

John Habyan asks me, "Anybody guys giving you stories about guys getting picked off and snapping?"

Bring it on, I'd love that.

"When Stump Merrill was manager, we used to get a lot of work in the bullpen. The kiss of death was you were definitely in there if he gave you the day off. He did it to Steve Farr a lot.

"This one day I went out there and pitched the eighth. I come in the dugout and I thought for sure I was going out there for the ninth because I knew Steve had the day off. I knew he was hangin'."

No he wasn't.

"Mark Connor says, 'No, no, we're bringing The Beast in.' I'm like, OK, this should be good. So he calls up Beast and Beast comes in for the ninth inning and just gets his lunch. He gives up the lead. He thought he had the day off and he was tired."

And now, it's showtime.

"He comes in the dugout and goes up to the phone hanging on the wall. You know how it has a metal case around it and the front door swings open? He opens the case, takes the receiver and rips it right off. He hangs it back up and then with the line dangling out, then he closes the case again.

"He doesn't say a word and walks out of the dugout."

Dave Righetti

2003 Makes it 20 Years

Nineteen eighty-three was the first full year Dave Righetti was getting the ball. And he got it on Independence Day to start against Boston at the Stadium.

The result was the Yankees' first regular-season no-hitter in 32 years.

"There were so many little side-plots that happened that day that I didn't realize until I was done because nobody talked to you. Nettles couldn't play because he had pink eye and he couldn't go outside. Willie Randolph didn't play either. Andre Robertson played second base. Donnie played first but at that time, he wasn't playing there fulltime. So we had some different people out there."

There was a reason for the substitutions.

"They had beaten us up for three straight days. I think maybe Billy decided to get to the All-Star break like, 'Let's just get out of here, rest up and go get them in the second half.'"

Righetti was too young to recognize he had something special warming up in the bullpen.

"At that age, I felt pretty good all the time. That was long before I started wearing my arm out. It was strange. I had trouble all day. I was throwing very hard that day, no question. Even my slider wasn't really going down. Occasionally it did, but it was really a hard one and stayed on the waist a lot, which is unusually high. I couldn't get it down because I was throwing it so hard. So I decided to use it more as cutter and I ran the ball underneath their hands instead of that down-and-in-the-dirt slider that Gator and Sparky had used all the time, something I was trying to perfect at that time."

Righetti, then, had just the one pitch effectively, his fastball.

"I had just pitched against those guys the start before in Boston. I was using all my pitches. I think I threw just one change-up, I might not have thrown one curveball, I threw all fastballs."

That command was missing in New York.

"In this game, I really didn't have great control. I just had this ball that was jumping around so I just stuck with it. I didn't force that slider down. Normally I would. I just let it go and it landed where it landed."

Of all the gin joints in the world, she had to walk into this one. Of all the hitters in the world, Wade Boggs stood between Dave Righetti and immortality.

"He was very hot. I think he was hitting .360-something. The last thing I thought about was striking him out. Twice during the game he hit balls to centerfield. I used to knock him down all the time, including that last at-bat. I always threw the ball in on him as hard as I could and just let him spray it off to the left. I'd get an easy strike and try to get him to at least give up on the plate a little bit and then use the slider on him. But I couldn't get the darn thing down and away to him. So I just used fastballs on him and Jerry Remy, who was also giving me trouble. On the last pitch, Butch Wynegar called for a slider and that was the right pitch. I had knocked him down and he had been frozen twice on pitches away already but Steve Palermo hadn't called it. I said, 'Well, I have to get this one down somehow.' I was tired enough I think that it went down. I aimed right in the ground when I threw it. I don't think it hit the ground. I

Dave Righetti

think Butch caught it in the air. That is my recollection. I just went, 'Geez, thank God this is over.'"

Race? What Race? Just Wake Me Up When It's Over

On the final day of the 1984 season, Don Mattingly and Dave Winfield staged their fight-to-the-finish show-down for the American League batting title. The Detroit Tigers, on their way to a World Championship, provided the weekend's opposition at the Stadium. Dave Righetti re-members something else from that final Sunday.

"Willie Hernandez is warming up for them which seemed odd given the circumstances. There was a van in center field that was used back then to ferry the relief pitch-ers into the game. It had a big Yankee emblem on the side. When they opened the double gates, the van would be sit-ting right there."

On this day, Bob Shirley was asleep in the front seat . . . just as Sparky Anderson went to the mound and made the motion for Hernandez.

"He's just snoring away and Hernandez is banging on the window yelling at him in Spanish. Shirley wakes up and goes, 'Hey, what's up?' The umpires are standing out there waiting for this van to start and bring him in. Well, Bob Shirley, instead of getting out and letting the regular guy drive in, he jumps over to the driver's seat and drives the van in with Hernandez."

In uniform.

"He drives the van around to the front of their dug-out, slams on the brakes and there's rocks flying everywhere.

Hernandez gets out and Shirley takes off and gives that smart-aleck little wave he used to do.

"I wished I was down there but I was down in the bullpen."

Steve Karsay

Dreams Do Come True

In his senior year at Christ the King High School in Queens, Steve Karsay played sandlot ball that summer for the Long Island Tigers.

Can you imagine being in high school and playing in Yankee Stadium?

"It was great being in Yankee Stadium for the first time and pitching off the mound. Going in there as a kid was a fun time. It's hard to explain, to go out to Monument Park to warm up in the Yankee bullpen to pitch on the field."

Karsay had been in the Stadium but had been unable to pitch.

"I had pitched two days before to get us to the championship game at Yankee Stadium. So I played first base. We ended up losing but it was still a thrill to be on the field and to play a seven-inning game there."

But it was still frustrating not being able to pitch.

"It was something that I wanted to do. I told my coach I was able to pitch an inning or two if he needed me. But that day was draft day and I actually got drafted on the day we played in Yankee Stadium. So even though we lost, it was still a great day for me."

Karsay was drafted 22nd overall in the 1990 draft by Toronto. A dozen years later, he is being introduced to the New York media in Yankee Stadium when GM Brian Cashman demonstrates a keen memory.

"He told me that he remembered seeing me play as a high school player at a tryout. I thought that was kind of neat that he could remember that far back and still know who exactly I was today."

Paying Admission

Playing for the Yankees in 2002 is Steve Karsay's fifth incarnation inside Yankee Stadium: as a child watching from the stands for the first time, with Christ the King, with the Long Island Tigers, as an opposition player and now pitching for the home team. He vividly remembers stage one.

"I wasn't able to get there as often as to Shea Stadium which was closer to my house. But to go to Yankee Stadium and to sit in the stands and knowing the guys who played there, Mickey Mantle, Joe DiMaggio, Babe Ruth, to have the aura of the stadium and the feeling of a baseball game with the New York Yankees in the pinstripes was special. I always wanted to go to Yankee games growing up. I relished every game I was able to go to there. I was 10 years old when I went there for the first time and they were playing the Boston Red Sox. I was in awe of what was around me and all the people that were there and what the Stadium meant."

Steve Karsay

Relieving Roger

Roger Clemens is going from Steve Karsay's idol to the guy he may relieve in 2002.

"Growing up I was a big baseball fan. I didn't root for any teams, I rooted for players that I really liked. I emulated certain people, and Roger Clemens was an idol of mine growing up. He was a rival of the New York Yankees. Now he is on the beloved New York Yankees. To actually sign and to know that Roger Clemens, a Hall of Famer, is gonna finish his career in New York and I'm gonna be able to be a part of watching him pitch and hopefully watching him get his 300th win is gonna be spine-tingling. It's a treat to play with so many great players and have a chance to win a World Series will be a lot of fun."

Jack Aker

Satchel

Jack Aker became the Yankee closer in 1969 and remained there until 1972, sharing the job with Lindy McDaniel and then being replaced by Sparky Lyle.

Aker came to the majors with the As in Kansas City in 1964. One year later, he became part of a boxscore for the ages. Aker finished the game that Satchel Paige started on September 25, 1965 . . . at the age of 59 years old or possibly a little younger.

Maybe only 57.

Nobody is quite sure.

"I don't know if we were told in advance that Satchel was coming, but I do remember when he walked into the room. At that time, players seemed to know the history of the game more than they do now and everybody, of course, had heard of Satchel Paige. We welcomed him."

Aker remembers Paige saying he would need a few days to get into shape to pitch. Finley planned to start him as a promotion called 'Light A Match for Satch Night.'

"We didn't really know if he was gonna pitch in a game or not but everyday he would come out and throw a little bit on the side. We had no idea how old he was but he had to be probably in his 60s. We watched him throw and he threw alright for a man that age. His control was impeccable. The catchers who warmed him up in the bullpen said they could sit in a rocking chair and catch him."

Speaking of rocking chairs, they brought one into the bullpen for Satchel.

"At that time, we didn't have a very good team so the stands weren't packed. But there was always a group of people who would buy tickets to come sit down by the bullpen to hear Satchel telling stories. He was a very friendly guy who would sit out there and also trade stories with us.

"The Red Sox are coming to town and they have a pretty good hitting club. The As were advertising that Satchel would start against them.

"He took the mound and three innings later he'd given up no runs and one hit. Carl Yastrzemski hit a double off of him to left-centerfield. It was an astounding event. He didn't throw extremely hard. I would guess he could still throw the ball 75 or 80 miles an hour. He threw harder in the game than he had on the sideline but his control was still amazing. He was cruising so easy he could have probably gone more than three innings. And the Red Sox were serious, they didn't let up."

But they did win the game 5-2. Satchel came out after three leading 1-0, giving the one hit and striking out one.

Pepi

"Joe Pepitone was a target of a lot of things that went on. Joe, at that time, had these hairpieces. He had one for off the field and another for on the field. Fans would remember that whenever Joe took off his batting helmet, he very quickly slipped his hat on all in one movement. The helmet came off, the hat went on. He would never be seen without one of these hairpieces. He was also the first guy to ever use a hair dryer in the clubhouse. We all took note of this. Joe would wait and shower by himself usually and then come out with his hairpiece on and proceed to blow-dry it and comb it all down. He was like a woman. He would spend an hour in front of the mirror."

Your attention please, ladies and gentlemen, now pitching for the Yankees, number 19, Fritz Peterson.

"Fritz loaded up Pepi's hair dryer with baby powder one night. At that time, we used to hang around the clubhouse a lot longer than the guys do now. Everybody was sitting around and we had already dressed. We were waiting for Pepi to get out of the shower. When he came out and he turned that hair dryer on, it looked a volcano went through the room. One of the funniest sights I ever saw, his whole upper body was snow white. We had guys rolling on the floor laughing so hard. I don't know if Joe actually was angry, but if it was an act, it was a good act. He was stomping and cussing and throwing things around. A few days later, he was laughing about it."

Ron Davis

A Real Pay Toilet

Goose Gossage heeded the call innings before he was expected to heed the call.

"It's 1980 and it was getting late in the ballgame. We were playing the Angels. It was about the sixth inning and Gossage went into the restroom. You have to put the door from the inside to get out."

Wouldn't you know it, there just happened to be a metal cable handy.

"I wrapped it around the door and tied it to the stairwell. Well, the phone rings and they say, 'Gossage, get up, get ready to throw.' Well, he jerked the door and that cable singed very tight. We couldn't get him out of the rest room. So they call back and say, 'RD, you get up.'"

While workmen were scouring the Stadium for a handy pair of wire-cutters to extricate the Goose, 'RD' was in the game on fire.

"I struck out all three in the eighth, got two outs in the ninth and Howser walks out in the ninth and pulls me. Goose comes in and gets the save."

Dick Howser fined Ron Davis $500 for his hijinks.

No Wonder They Run in From the Bullpen

"We were in Milwaukee. They'd drive you in from the bullpen in a Firebird around the pads and stop and you'd get out and run to the mound. They called down to get Gossage up to start the ninth inning."

The Yanks are out and it's time for a Goose with a twist.

"He walks down to the car. You usually get in on the passenger side. He opens the door on the driver's side and takes the driver out of the car. He get in the car, closes the door, turns up the radio, revs up the engine, the wheels are spinning and there's rocks shooting out from underneath and there's smoke. Right before he hits the grass, he does a left turn and just floors it all the way around right field until he gets in front of the first-base dugout which was Milwaukee's."

By this time, Davis estimates Gossage is probably going 45 to 50.

"He hits the brakes and starts a skid of about 30 feet on the side on the rocks. Dust and gravel is flying into their dugout. He comes out and there's smoke everywhere and the engine's throbbing. He jumps out of the car, runs out to the mound, throws nine pitches, strikes three guys out, game over."

Steve Howe

Number 57 in Your Program

From the beginning of his career until the end, Steve Howe wore uniform number 57. A cut number.

"When I went to spring training in 1980, I told my wife and everyone that I got invited to early spring camp. I said I was going there to make the club. When I got down there, that was what they gave the batting practice pitchers and rookies and stuff."

Howe was true to his word.

"When I made the club, they said, 'OK, you get a good new number now, kid.' I said, 'For what? A number doesn't make the athlete. The athlete makes the number. They'll remember it one way or another.' And they did."

A Dream Fulfilled

Steve Howe was on the Stadium mound long before he became a Yankee in 1991. Ten years earlier, he was busy nailing down the final outs in the Dodgers' six-game victory in the 1981 World Series.

"The biggest thing for me personally as an athlete was to be able to go to the next level. For me to be involved in two saves and one win in the World Series not only was special but that it came against the New York Yankees. The New York Yankees are an icon on sports. They are 'the' sports franchise. They have the oldest tradition with Scooter, Thurman Munson, Reggie Jackson, Mickey, Billy, all those people, you automatically go, 'Yankees.' To beat them was even bigger because we weren't supposed to. We were the kids."

Every kid dreams of the moment Howe experienced.

"For me, it's the pinnacle for an athlete is to win a World Championship. Great, great, great players who I respect very much, Mr. Cub, Ernie Banks, all those guys never got a World Championship. And they deserved it. There's only one thing in my life that I ever experienced that was any higher than that moment. That was when my children were born healthy."

Beating the Door Down

It took persistence for Steve Howe to become a Yankee.

"Peter Ueberroth had basically blacklisted me when he was Commissioner. So I went to Japan and to Mexico. I had had an arm surgery and I was playing winter ball. I had taken my family down there during the Gulf War. We couldn't come home because of that. When I finally did, my agent, Dick Moss, was talking to Gene Michael, who was the Yankee GM."

Howe says Michael promised his agent a tryout. "We checked with scouts and he really wasn't throwing that well," Michael reportedly said.

"That's how it always goes. Then all of sudden he went cold on us. He wouldn't return Dick's phone calls and spring training had already started. I had put all my eggs in one basket, to go with the Yankees."

And because he had, Howe took matters into his own hands.

"Cindy and I took money we did not have, bought plane tickets to fly down to Fort Lauderdale and went up to Gene's door. When Dick Moss walked in, Gene came out and Dick said, 'We're here.' And Gene said, 'What are you doing here?' And Dick said, 'You were gonna give Steve a shot.' Howe says Gene said, 'I never said that. Get in my office.' They went in the office and Cindy and I stood outside the office. We took a 100% chance. About twenty minutes later, Stick says, 'You have your cleats and your glove with you?' I said, 'Yep.' He said, 'Come on out and throw.' Once he saw me, and I was throwing 94 miles per hour, he said, 'Come back again tomorrow. Can you do that again?'

Howe told Michael he was a little bit stiff.

"I came back the next day and threw harder. I signed that day. I was never invited. I just showed up."

Steve Howe earned a minor league contract and began the 1991 season in Triple-A Columbus where he recorded five saves. He was promoted in May and immediately became the big club's most effective reliever, pitching to a 1.68 ERA.

Loaded for Bear

In 1996, just after his release from the Yankees brought his career to an end, Steve Howe thought he was on his way home to Montana. Instead, he was arrested at JFK Airport and charged with carrying a concealed handgun in a carry-on bag aboard a plane. Howe says he did no such thing.

"The gun wasn't mine. It was never on a carry-on. No one knows that the wife of a friend of mine who is a policeman in New York and my wife packed that gun. It was in my wife's locked suitcase. I had no knowledge it was even there. They knew it was me and they arrested me. So once again, I ate it. I'm a lot more stand-up guy than people think."

Kathy

Steve Howe lost his beloved sister to cancer. She was 39.

"It's still hard to talk about because I miss her. She was a little over 13 months younger than me. She is the only person in my life I never had an argument with. She was always my fragile little sister and I always tried to take care of her. We were joined at the hip. What she meant to me was no judgment and unselfish love. I had to go and be with her and watch someone who was as precious to me as life itself die. The helplessness that I felt made me a ten-times better person because you know what, we're not here to like everybody and we're not here to be treated well by everybody. But we can still make a difference by liking everybody who is likable. And we can make a huge difference by treating people the way we wanted to be treated. And that is the way my sister was."

3
CATCHERS

Johnny Ellis

Johnny Ellis, a strong-as-bull catcher in the late 60s, was afflicted with Hodgkin's Disease. Now cancer-free for 15 years, he has taken darkness and transformed it into light.

"The issues that surrounded my decision to turn my problem around was quite simply this. My brother and sister had died of cancer, one from Hodgkins, the other from lymphoma both before the age of 40. Subsequently, before I was 40, I was diagnosed with Hodgkins, stage four. At stage five, there is not too much hope."

Ellis' doctor performed what he called "medical protocol", a fancy term for experimentation.

"While sitting in this dark room thinking about what I have missed in life, I really couldn't think of anything else and that's the truth. Not expecting to live, I really didn't use any mind therapy that patients use to fight cancer."

That's when Johnny Ellis made a commitment.

"I made a deal with whoever you make a deal with while you have tubes in you and a bunch of other stuff because I had had a few operations during this period of time. I said, 'Lookit, if I get a chance to live I'm going to help needy cancer families and also fund cancer research.' So not expecting to live, I thought it was a fair deal."

Ellis had seen the devastating financial effects of the disease close-up.

"During that period of time when my brother went through his bout with cancer, he was a teacher in our school system in Connecticut. His insurance limits reached their ceilings and subsequently, he did not have enough money to fight cancer. So as a family, we had to put money in to help his fight, things like paying for his home and taking care of his medicines. So I really felt that there was a need."

As Johnny Ellis began to survive and get his treatments for cancer, he saw other people far worse off than he was. They did not have the financial wherewithal to fight the disease.

"People afflicted with cancer who are the breadwinners in the family, if they don't have enough money to pay their bills, the psychological build-up, the piling-on of your problems become greater sometimes than your will to live. And this is, in itself, a problem in fighting cancer.

"If you wanted me to weigh the percentage of lifesaving force versus the financial benefit or treatment, I'd have to say that having the financial strength is equal to getting the best treatment possible."

Ellis says a lot of people were compromised under this pressure.

"I was going through this treatment and seeing all these people collapsing under this pressure, people who were not coming back the next day. So as I began to survive my own therapy to treat my cancer, I went out and formed a foundation."

This is long before that became commonplace for contemporary athletes.

"I asked Mickey Mantle, Whitey Ford and Billy Martin to come to my first dinner. We raised $150,000."

That was in the late 80s. Since then, Johnny Ellis has raised in the vicinity of four or five million dollars.

"I made a pact with whoever you make you pact with. I said I better live up to it."

Literally.

Johnny Oates

While Johnny Oates was a back-up catcher with the Yankees, Graig Nettles was diagnosed with hepatitis.

"We were in Minnesota and they informed the team we were all gonna have to go down and get injected to prevent the rest of the team from getting it. We were bused to a clinic in downtown Minneapolis where we all got in line."

Cue Yogi.

"We were all going through to get our shots and Yogi asks, 'How much do these things cost?' One of the nurses says, 'Well, Mr. Berra, they're free.' He says, 'Well, in that case, give me two of them.'

"That was your normal Yogi take on things."

Don't Believe What You Hear

Johnny Oates holds no illusions. He knew his place on the Yankee squad.

"I was one of those guys who was the 26th guy on a 25-man ballclub.

"In 1981, I was supposed to go to Columbus as a player/coach. That was the plan when I went to spring training. But with injuries to Bruce Robinson, who came up with a rotator cuff tear, I ended up making the big league club right out of spring training."

That last night of spring training, Gene Michael told Johnny Oates he had made the club.

"I'm going through the players parking lot and George came up to me, took my hand and wished me well in Columbus. He did not know that I had already been told that I had made the ballclub. I guess he was trying to get my goat a little bit. But I caught on to him real quick. It was probably the only time in my life that I've ever been half a step ahead of George Steinbrenner."

The '81 club opened at home against Texas for three games, went to Toronto for three and then to Texas, where circumstances intervened.

"I think it was a Friday night in Texas and Rick Cerone, the starting catcher, broke his thumb. I went from a player/coach in Triple-A to the starting catcher for the New York Yankees in a matter of a few days.

"I was thrilled."

Yet, Oates was brutally realistic about his state in life.

"I couldn't play anymore and they knew that before they even started me. But I had to start four or five days in a row until they picked up Barry Foote. He came in, had a great April and I was released when Cerone came off the DL.

"It was quite a story for me coming off the garbage heap to the starting catcher for the New York Yankees."

Jerry Narron

A Night Like None Other

Thurman Munson died in a plane crash on a Thursday, August 2, 1979, an off-day for the Yankees. The Baltimore Orioles arrived for a weekend series that night.

On Friday night, in one of the most emotional scenes in the Stadium's grand history, eight players took the field. It fell upon rookie Jerry Narron to do the catching. He was still in shock over the tragic death of the Yankee captain:

"Ron Davis and I were living together in Dumont, New Jersey. I believe Catfish called us."

That's like one of those moments where you drop the phone.

"Absolutely."

But there were games to be played.

"I got to the Stadium Friday afternoon and everybody was just heartbroken. Before the game they told me that for the National Anthem they were gonna leave home plate vacant and that there would be a moment of silence."

Narron was told to go out on the field after that.

"I will never forget that night. I don't know if I'll ever be in a situation as difficult to play or perform or compete in a game as that was for me."

But perform he did.

"I think one thing about all professional athletes and that we're trying to focus on the competition at that moment we're playing and I think it helped me through that game. I think it helped everybody on our club through that game."

Times change but circumstances don't.

"I think that attitude has helped everybody over the last few months that are professional athletes after what happened on September 11."

Munson's passing was the death-knell for the Yankees' season. Ask Jerry Narron how he got through those ensuing days and weeks and he says, "I don't think our club did at all. I think it took until the next season for them to recover. I got traded that winter but I really believe that after Thurman got killed, we had no chance of winning the rest of the way."

Unforgettable

There are two special people in Jerry Narron's baseball life.

"One is Johnny Oates and the other is Catfish Hunter. With Catfish, when I made the club in '79, I was not married and was there by myself. He let me move in with him until his family got there in June. I mean he really showed me the ropes of how it was to be a major league player."

And then there was this about Catfish.

"The first time I was gonna catch him in the big leagues we were playing the Orioles at home. I was gonna go over the club with him and he said, 'Don't worry about it, I'm gonna throw every pitch you call for. If I don't like it, I'll just throw it so they can't hit it.' That was just unbelievable, to show what kind of guy he is, working with a young catcher and taking full responsibility like that."

Rick Cerone

A Real-Life 99-pound Weakling

"I wrestled my freshman year at Essex Catholic High School in New Jersey. I was five feet tall and 99 pounds. My father said eventually I was gonna grow, wrestling is a tough sport and said maybe I should find something else. My best friend is growing up came from a fencing family. So we played football, baseball and we fenced. I got into fencing, enjoyed it and became a state champion in New Jersey. One of my teammates was Peter Westbrook, who fenced in the Olympics. I actually did a little bit in college at Seton Hall as well. All because I was a five-foot, 99-pound weakling as a freshman in high school."

Bad Reception

After high school, Rick Cerone received a tryout from the Yankees which was held at the Stadium in the summer of 1972.

"I was playing American Legion ball and we had played a night game the night before. I went back down to the Jersey shore to a summer house that all the Cerones went to. At about 9 o'clock in the morning, we got a phone call from a local scout saying, 'Rick, if you want, there's a tryout for the Yankees but you have to be at the Stadium by 11 o'clock.'"

On this day, Rick's father was off from work.

"He said, 'Let's go.' And then we realized we had no uniform. The only uniform we had was my Legion uniform

Rick Cerone

that was being washed. So we had to take it out of the washing machine."

Now picture this.

"On the way up the Garden State Parkway trying to dry it out, we had it hanging on the antenna of the car. People were looking at it. There was a jock, there's the underwear, there's the uniform. They thought we were crazy. To be honest with you, over that hour drive up to Yankee Stadium, the uniform did not completely dry. So when I got there, I was all excited. There were about 250 high school players and some college players. But I guarantee you I was the only one in a wet, wet uniform."

But it was clean.

Cliff Johnson

Buckle Your Seatbelts, It's Going to Be a Bumpy Ride

Cliff Johnson was being dealt to a great 1977 club, the New York Yankees.

"It was really horrible the way the Astros traded me. They traded me getaway night, which was also the trading deadline. That night we had a game in the Astrodome against the Mets. After the game, we were gonna open up a seven-game road swing with three games in New York and four games in Montreal. They don't tell me before our charter leaves. They tell me when we're about 18,000 feet in the air. Bob Lillis, who was a coach, comes back to tell me that the skipper wants to see me up front. I go up to see what he wants and Bill Virdon looks through these horn-rimmed glasses with this look on his face and tells me that I'm a Yankee now."

In trading him in the manner in which they did, Johnson said that nullified his 72-hour period to report.

"I spent the night in the hotel with the Astros but I was going to the opposite side of town. I was kind of in awe when I joined the Yankees. When Gabe Paul picked me up at the hotel that morning after we had breakfast, we took a cab up to Yankee Stadium. I had never been there before. I'm a kid off the west side of San Antonio. I had never been to the Bronx. I met Billy Martin for the first time. Billy was very cordial and warm and his old cunning self when he needed to be. And here was there 650-pound gorilla sitting behind this large, gorgeous desk by the name of George Steinbrenner. He was also very cordial and nice. One of the first things he asked me was if I had my bats. I told them I was sure they went over at Shea Stadium. He sent somebody over to get my bats. He asked me what size shoes I wore. He had shoes brought in. He's sitting behind this desk pressing buttons. I'm going, wow, this guy is like the President of the United States or something."

Balms Away

"What Sparky Lyle pulled on Yogi was a classic. Every night after a ballgame was over, Yogi would use Sparky's toothpaste. Knowing Count the way he was, and he was a great prankster anyway, he said he was gonna get even with

Yogi. He took some of that analgesic balm and put it into the tube of toothpaste. I think that stopped Yogi from borrowing Sparky's toothpaste."

Ron Hassey

Meet the Babe

Ruth wasn't the only lefthanded hitter the Yankees called "Babe."

"The name came about when we were playing in Baltimore. Butch Wynegar got hurt and I went into the ballgame that night and proceeded to go 0-for-4. The next night I got another start and I hit two home runs. Earl Weaver commented in the paper, "Who does Hassey think he is, Babe Ruth?" That kind of stuck with me.

Ironic that it happened in the city where the Babe, the original, was born and raised.

Hello, Goodbye, Hello, Goodbye, Hello, Goodbye

Read any good resumes lately of any players traded twice by the same team to the same team?

"It started when I was traded from the Cubs to the Yankees in '85. At the end of the season, I was traded to the Chicago White Sox. Just before spring training started, I got traded back to the Yankees. Then in the middle of the '86 season, I was traded back to the White Sox. During that time I was injured. I had a bad knee. There, I finished out the season. After the '87 season, I think it was, I became a free agent and almost signed back with the Yankees. Instead, I went with the Oakland As."

All the movement did not sit well with Hassey.

"It kind of was very frustrating because I really enjoyed playing in New York. I finally found a place that I really liked. I liked the big-city atmosphere. The fans of New York were outstanding to me. I had a good year there. I had a pretty good season in '85 and I was really looking forward to the '86 season. Then I went back and forth and when it happened again in the middle of the season, the second time was very frustrating. There was no time to think about it."

4
INFIELDERS

Frank Tepedino

The Events of 9/11

Frank Tepedino has served the City of New York as a firefighter after playing in the majors in 1967 and again from '69 to '75. His two sons followed and a brother are also in the FDNY.

"My one son is coming in from working a 24-hour tour but my brother is on vacation. I turn on the TV and I see the fire. He said, 'Did you hear about the plane that went into the Trade Center?' I said, 'Oh my God, you've got to be kidding me.' I remember being a little kid and reading about the plane that hit the Empire State Building in '46. I said, 'Not again.' It's kind of unusual for a small plane to be off course like that. When we were watching it, we found out a big jetliner went into it. But we still didn't believe that it was terrorism until the second one hit.

"I knew my other son was going in to work later that day. I had to make sure he was OK. We just jumped in a car and all headed in with two other guys we picked up on the way. We got in there as soon as we could. We had no problem getting in."

By this time, the World Trade Center was gone.

"It was just on such a massive scale, it was unreal. We were there for about 38 hours straight. I lost one kid from our firehouse. There had to be a good 50, 60 others, easy, that I knew by name and probably about 150 by sight.

"Emotionally, it was like a loss in the family but then it goes a little bit further. It's the camaraderie of the job. I've always said it's like being a part of a team. It's the loss that was so senseless."

Reaching out . . . finally

Last fall, Frank Tepedino was selected by the Yankees to throw out the first ball prior to one of their Divisional Series playoff games against Oakland. He found it ironic.

"It was funny because I hadn't heard from the Yankees in 30 years. I thought somebody was just fooling around. There were so many reporters calling, so many news articles about the kid we had lost. When I got the call to throw out the first pitch, I was like, sure, OK. And then to get to the ballpark and to know that you're gonna part of something like that for the kid we had lost."

It was special to Tepedino because he felt like he was acting on someone else's behalf.

"The kid we had lost was such a big Yankee fan. We invited his mom and dad and his brothers and his sister to the game that night. Everyone knew the reason I was walking out to the mound to throw out the first pitch was because of this kid. It gave them a little bit of solace about losing their son. Here you are in the middle of America's pastime and his name was mentioned. The family really, really appreciated something like that. So it meant a lot."

Spike Owen

Spike Own preceded his University of Texas teammate, Roger Clemens, to the home team clubhouse in the Bronx. After playing four years in Montreal, Owen became a free agent after the 1992 season. He signed a three-year contract with the Yankees and started the home opener at shortstop.

"We opened up on the road that year in Cleveland and then went to Chicago before we came home. The atmosphere in parks like Yankee Stadium is so unique and hard to beat with the history and all the great players and all the ghosts. I'm very well aware of all that stuff. Running out on the field and looking up was an amazing feeling.

"To see the Stadium jam-packed for a beautiful day game even when I talk about it now, it still gives me goosebumps to think I was out there and part of that game."

Owen was very nervous but less so once he got out there.

"I got a ground ball in the first inning which helped. I was batting ninth as usual. The big moment for me was my first time up in the second or third inning and I got a base hit in my first at bat in Yankee Stadium as a Yankee. That's a fond memory."

That gave Owen approximately 56,000 new best friends.

"I feel so fortunate in my career that I got to wear the pinstripes and play in Yankee Stadium. Unfortunately, I didn't get to spend all three of those years there and was traded to California. Being able to play in that ballpark as a Yankee is just hard to describe."

Good thing he didn't drop that first ball. As Rodney Dangerfield says, "It's a tough crowd."

East is East and West is West

Like most players, Spike Owen's career was spread out through different teams. From Seattle to Boston to Montreal to New York to California. He has always had difficulty telling friends back home in Austin, Texas that there is a profound difference in attitude.

"I got to experience a lot of teams, on the West Coast and on the East Coast and I even got to experience Montreal, another country. It is hard to put into words what East Coast baseball is like, Red Sox fans and Yankee fans. It is very intense, pressure-packed on every pitch. You can go from getting booed after one pitch or one groundball to being a hero in the very next at-bat if you do your job, whether it's a basehit or bunt or sac fly. Then they're back with you. There's a lot to that. The thing is, man, they care. They want their team to win. There's no other place like it. They actually come to that ballpark and expect you to win and you better show up to play."

That's what Owen tried to explain to people.

"We are professionals. You're getting paid to play the game. But there is a different mentality when you suit up with the pinstripes and go out and play in Yankee Stadium. I honestly believe ballplayers didn't approach things any differently when I played in Seattle or California. I know I certainly wasn't trying any less out there. But it's an intensity that's in the ballpark pretty much day in and day out. And you are aware of that."

Cletis Boyer

Learning From the Master

In 1994, Derek Jeter of the Columbus Clippers was named the Minor League Player of the Year. Problem was he was experiencing fielding problems, specifically, throwing problems. He made a staggering 54 errors.

Flip ahead to spring training, 1995, replacement player spring training. Enter one of the best ever to put an infielder's glove on, Cletis Boyer, coaching in spring training.

"I'm watching Derek work out. Every ground ball hit to him, he was looking the ball into his glove and his glove, most of the time, was going through his legs. Then he would come up and throw."

Boyer told Jeter that he must have made an error and somebody told him to look the ball into his glove. Jeter said that was the case.

"For a year and a half, he was following the ball into his glove. Somebody told me he was throwing a lot of balls up into the seats. He made 25 or 30 errors throwing."

Boyer said "we had about six instructors in the organization teaching that didn't know how to teach. We had six instructors that never had one day of pro ball. So how the hell could you teach a kid how to play?"

Boyer said to Jeter, "I'm gonna ask you a question and I'm not gonna trick you. Where are you trying to throw to the first baseman, what area? He said, 'Chest high.' I said, 'Oh. With your arm, you're gonna throw chest high? If you leave the ball up a tiny bit, it's your error.'"

Boyer knew about first base play. As an active player, he used to take grounders there. He then imparted his wisdom.

"I want you to throw the ball to my waist. But if you miss me, miss me low or miss me in. I can actually catch it on the ground and I can tag him in."

In five weeks taking throws at first, Derek Jeter never pulled Clete Boyer off of first down the right field line. He threw three balls over his head that he didn't have to jump for.

Boyer told him, "Just try to keep low. If the ball is hit at you, just try to have your glove on the ground first," which he does.

Clete Boyer says everyone in the organization wanted to move Derek Jeter to the outfield. Meanwhile, he was making this bold assertion.

"Honest to God, I said before he ever played in the big leagues that he was gonna be the greatest Yankee shortstop ever. He is. You can see it. He could have been in the big leagues the next week. That's all he needed."

Think about the tutor every time you see Derek Jeter field a ball.

Degrees of Separation

Clete Boyer, Carney Lansford, Wade Boggs, Scott Brosius. Boyer had a profound effect on them all, transforming each into Gold Glove-caliber third basemen. The tutorials started when Boyer and Lansford were with Oakland.

"I said I'm gonna talk to you in spring training about infield. Carney was the most serious guy I've ever seen. He was like Mattingly. He was unbelievable. He came to spring training. I got him down and open and stretching with those hamstrings. You gotta be like a rubber band. He told me later he had to crawl up and down the stairs because his hamstrings were so tight. People don't stretch their hamstrings out. In other words, you can't get down low."

Years later in Oakland, Lansford taught Brosius how to play the way Boyer years prior taught him.

"I'll tell you the biggest thrill I had in spring training last year. It was talking to Scott Brosius. I loved that guy. You see how he plays? He said to me, 'Are you the guy who taught Carney Lansford how to play third?' I said, 'Yeah.'"

Boyer had just one question for Brosius.

"When you charge the ball that you have to bare-hand and throw on the run, I want to know where you're trying to throw the ball. He said, 'I have to throw the ball five or six feet on the inside of first.' A lot of people make that play but hit the runner or throw it away because of your momentum going in. The three years I was there, I never saw him screw that play up."

While Brosius was in Oakland, Boggs was winning his first Gold Glove with the Yankees.

"Honest to God, Boggs will tell you, I never talked to him in front of anybody. I never told him he had to do this.

When he came to us, he was a stand-up third baseman. And when your feet are close together, you can't go to your right and you can't dive to you right."

Oh, you can dive.

"You can dive, but the ball is 30 feet by you by the time you hit the ground.

"Chipper Jones is the worst right now. His hands are up above his knees. So how's he gonna catch balls down the line? He has to move his right foot first for his left foot to cross over. He can't do it."

Which is why the Braves are moving him to left field for the 2002 season.

Joe Pepitone

Just Put it Right There, Pal

Nobody has ever denied that Denny McLain did not groove a pitch for Mickey Mantle to hit home run #535 and surpass Jimmy Foxx. Joe Pepitone was the on-deck hitter. Here's what he saw.

"I was batting fourth, Mickey is batting third. They were beating us something like 11-3 in the ninth inning and Mantle's coming up to bat for the last time. McLain calls his catcher, Bill Freehan, out to the mound to say something to him. I think Mickey was 0-for-3 that game."

Freehan went behind the plate and Mickey stepped in.

Joe Pepitone

"The next thing you know, McLain's first pitch is right down the middle. He just wound up easy and threw it. Mickey was like shocked. So Mickey looked at McLain and he pointed with his hand to throw it a little further outside."

Pepitone is on-deck watching this in disbelief.

"I'm thinking what the hell is going on here? The next pitch is right down the middle again, a nice, easy fastball that Mickey pops it up to the catcher. Freehan just stood there watching it bounce. I'm just looking at this amazed. So Mickey looks out at McLain again. He has two strikes on him. He said with his hands again to throw it a little further outside. Sure as hell, he throws it right down the middle and Mickey hits a line drive off the third deck that was headed for the roof at Tiger Stadium. Mickey's just running around the bases and everybody was shaking his hand."

McLain came to home plate and he's standing there with Pepitone waiting to congratulate Mantle.

"I'm asking McLain if he's still in a good mood. He's not saying anything to me. Mickey comes home and McLain shakes his hand, Freehan shakes his hand, I shake his hand and McLain goes out to the mound."

Pepitone decides he'll be the one to give McLain the signs.

"I look at McLain and I point like I want a fastball straight ahead. He shakes his head no. I give him the curve motion and he says no."

That's when Denny McLain wound up, easily threw the pitch behind him and hit Joe Pepitone right in the helmet.

"I said look at that son-of-a-bitch. That's what they do for those guys who hit all those home runs. Mickey was on the bench laughing his ass off."

And Step on it Cabbie

Another Detroit story.

"Phil Linz and I are rookies. We were just finished eating in this restaurant and we see Mantle and Ford in the lounge. They called us over."

They were impressed that these two gods wanted to talk to them.

"They tell us they're gonna go out to this place called The Flame Lounge after we eat. They say, 'Why don't you guys go there, we'll tell you where it is and we'll meet you there.' The cab ride was about $35. That was our meal money."

And that cab took them directly to The Flame Lounge, conveniently located in the heart of what was then the Detroit slums.

"It had these little round portholes on this brick building. I looked in and could see it was a bad, bad place. I see all these guys laying on the bar. I walked in."

No, he didn't just walk in. Joe Pepitone had an announcement to make.

"I say, 'I'm Joe Pepitone of the New York Yankees. I'm supposed to meet Mr. Whitey Ford and Mr. Mickey Mantle here.' People just looked at me. One guy says, 'You better get out of here before you get yourselves killed.' We realize they played a joke on us. So we take another cab back for another $35.

"I tell Phil, 'Listen, when we get on the bus to go to the ballpark tomorrow, let me do the talking.' Just as I get on, I see Mickey in the back and I say, 'Mickey, I couldn't get there last night with Phil. I had to come home and call my mother.' He says, 'You're full of crap. We saw you there. We were sitting in the back. We saw you come in.' He was full of crap. They just sent us on a wild goose-chase. That's what they used to do."

Steve Balboni

Waiting a Lifetime

Steve Balboni will never forget his first major league at-bat.

"It was pretty intimidating. That 1981 team was almost like an All-Star team. It was a great team to be part of."

Balboni was getting advanced billing. He had heard that Phil Rizzuto and Frank Messer were building him up, talking about him on radio and TV while he was still in the minor leagues.

"I don't remember how many people were there. It seemed like a million. There was a good crowd there and it seemed incredibly loud.

"I remember walking up to the plate and it was so loud, I couldn't believe it. On every pitch, it seemed to get louder."

Balboni faced fellow rookie Howard Bailey of Detroit and all 6-3, 225 pounds of him hit a triple. With that blinding speed?

"With that big ballpark. I hit it about 425 feet and it didn't go out."

I Wanna Be a Part of It, New York, New York

Steve Balboni would have loved to have played his entire career in New York.

"I had a great experience, too, in Kansas City. We won a World Series there and the people there were excellent. We lived there for eight years. Even though I knew it was gonna be tougher to break into the line-up with the Yankees and I was going to Kansas City to play every day, it was tough. I still had mixed feelings when I got traded."

You never forget the ghosts.

"I enjoyed being part of that tradition, the way they go about things. Watching them on TV the last few years, watching the way they play, it's like this is what it's all about. I've seen other teams and been on other teams where it's just not the same. It's almost like it's an effort for people to go out there. Guys really don't care as much. I played in Seattle before they sold the team and things were turned around there. It was unbelievable. We lost like nine games in a row and nobody seemed to care from the front office down."

Based on that experience, Balboni says there is no place like New York.

"I don't think there is any team like New York. Winning is important. That's what makes it more fun and that's the way I felt about baseball."

How about this for an epilogue?

"The one thing I liked was nobody was bigger than the pinstripes. Everybody had the same goal and if you weren't for the team, you weren't there very long."

Chris Chambliss

Welcome to New York

It was a shock when the Yankees broke up a clique when they traded four pitchers to Cleveland in April, 1974 for Chris Chambliss, Dick Tidrow and Cecil Upshaw.

It was also jarring to Chambliss who was going the other way. He had inadvertently gone out in a blaze of glory.

"We were home playing the Angels and had the bases loaded in the eighth inning against Nolan Ryan. I think we were down by about two runs. I hit a line-drive down the leftfield line that cleared the bases. It was exciting because it put us ahead. We played one more inning and we won. We're in the clubhouse and everybody's jumping up and down because it celebration time."

And then it suddenly got quiet.

"Ken Aspromonte, who was also my Triple-A manager, was our manager. He had replaced Alvin Dark. He called me into the office. He really liked me a lot but he had a sad look on his face. Dick Tidrow and Cecil Upshaw were already in there."

And then it happened.

"He told us we were traded. This is a Friday night. I was shocked. I come out of his office and the celebration has cooled. It was a large trade because it was a seven-player deal and they were getting four pitchers back. At that time, Cleveland didn't have a lot of pitching, but we had a lot of good hitting."

The very next morning, Chambliss was on a plane bound for New York.

Chris Chambliss

"I think it was a one o'clock game and I was in a Yankee uniform at Shea Stadium. It was just a severe shock."

Gone!

Here is Chris Chambliss' description of one of the biggest home runs in Yankee history.

"I knew I hit it deep. It was one of those ones that was hit high and it was hit not too far from the wall, really. It didn't go over by very much.

"McRae went to the wall looking like it might come down in his glove but it went just over that fence. It wasn't one of those that you hit and you know that it is gone. The one like that that I really enjoyed was my World Series home run. When I hit that, I knew it was gone. This one, I didn't know it was gone."

9/11

Chris Chambliss, having completed his season as the Marlins' Triple-A manager in Calgary, was invited to Florida to join the major league coaching staff for the final month of the 2001 season.

He had an early morning flight from Newark to Fort Lauderdale on Tuesday, September 11. That means he may possibly have been in the take-off line in front of United Flight 93, one of the doomed planes that was to be commandeered by hijackers that crashed near Shanksville, Pennsylvania at 10:10 a.m.

"The flight was somewhere around 8:15. While we're up in the air, a lady right behind me is looking out the window on the left-hand side that faces the Manhattan skyline. I turned around and she said that the World Trade Center was smoking."

At that point, Chambliss and his fellow passengers had no idea about the mayhem that was going on.

"A little later on in the flight, the pilot told us that we were going to land in Durham. He assured us it was nothing mechanical and said he would explain more when we landed."

Chambliss was instructed to get his luggage out of baggage claim and leave the airport premises as soon as possible. A phone call home told him all he needed to know about the worst terrorist attack ever on American soil.

"I got a hotel room, stayed there three days, and was in touch with the team. They were to play home games on the 11th, 12th and 13th and then play in Atlanta over the weekend. If they were gonna play those games, I was gonna rent a car and drive there from Durham."

Of course, those games were postponed too.

"Once we found that out, I rented a car anyway and drove north back home to New Jersey. Just so happened my parents live in Alexandria, Virginia, so I drove about five hours to their house and stayed with them for the weekend. Then I drove home."

By this time, the season was resuming.

"The Marlins started up in Montreal. It would have been impossible to get there through international flying. After there, they were to go to Philadelphia which was only a train ride away for me. That's what I did later that week to meet the club and ended up spending the rest of the season with them."

Chris Chambliss puts it all in perspective this way:

"The ordeal was nothing was compared to what everybody else went through. I was just very fortunate."

Safe at Home . . . Wherever it May Be

In the wake of the pandemonium that greeted Chris Chambliss' pennant-winning home run, everything on the Stadium that could be taken was. That included home plate.

"The first thing that happened was when I came around second base. I tripped right after I hit the bag. I don't know why, I just tripped. I quickly got back up."

It's not every day one worries about getting trampled after one hits a home run.

"People were all over the place. I remember, and I've seen a picture of it, someone trying to grab my helmet. I don't know what made me do it but I grabbed my helmet and tucked it away like a football. Third base was just a mob of people so I kind of went around them toward the outfield and just swung around in front of the Royals dugout. I was in a full sprint then straight into our dugout. I was just dodging people. I just remember somebody in front of me that I must have forearmed or something and just stepped over him and headed to the dugout."

And the clubhouse where everybody asked him if he ever touched home plate.

"I said no way did I touch it because there were a bunch of people around. Nobody hardly knows this, but I put on a jacket and took two security cops in uniform and the three of us went through the crowd. While people were still jumping around near home plate, I put my foot on the area where it was. No umpire saw it but we did it anyway and went back in the clubhouse. It was really wild."

Frank Verdi

A Real-Life Moonlight Graham

Remember toward the end of "Field of Dreams" when Kevin Costner is sitting in a room with Burt Lancaster, who's playing a former big leaguer named Moonlight Graham who never got a chance to hit? He laments that he wishes he had just had one at-bat.

This is the amazing story of 26-year-old rookie Frank Verdi of Brooklyn, New York in his eighth year of professional baseball.

"I'm in Boston and it's May 10, 1953. Back then, we left spring training before there was a final cutdown on May 15, so we had about 30 players. On his day, like any other, I took infield and batting practice and put my glove in the locker room never figuring I would get in the game."

"It must have been about the sixth inning and we're losing 3-1. Rizzuto was due to hit and Stengel said, 'Mize, you hit for Rizzuto.' So Mize pinch-hits. After the inning, he said, 'Verdi, you play short.' I almost fell over. I didn't have my glove there so I had to go running inside."

Verdi was now at shortstop for Rizzuto.

"Raschi was pitching and retired the Sox. In the next inning, we batted around. We had tied it up at 3-3 and had the bases loaded. I was in Rizzuto's lead-off spot. I remember Stengel yelling to me, 'Butcher boy, butcher boy.' That was one of his favorite expressions for chopping down at the ball. I think Ellis Kinder was pitching. He walked Raschi to force in a run and give the Yankees a 4-3 lead."

Verdi was next.

"I walk into the batter's box and the next thing I heard is 'Time out.' One of the coaches, Bill McKechnie, comes out to the mound and the next thing I know, they wave to the bullpen and change pitchers."

Verdi backs out of the batter's box.

"When the pitcher got through taking his warm-up pitches, I walked back into the batters box again. As I'm getting ready to hit, I hear, 'Time out' again. I said, 'What the hell is this now?' Stengel had called time out and I turned around and there was Bill Renna swinging three bats and loosening up. He came up to bat to pinch-hit for me."

Three days later, Frank Verdi was farmed out to Syracuse, never to return to the major leagues. He is listed, however, in the *Baseball Encyclopedia*.

You can't make this stuff up.

Ken Phelps

So Do How Does it Feel to be the Punchline?

The 1988 trade of Jay Buhner for Ken Phelps was immortalized on 'Seinfeld' when the character played by Jerry Stiller excoriates 'George Steinbrenner' saying, "How could you trade Jay Buhner?"

"To me, I have kind of learned to laugh it off. It's more important to be remembered for something than to not be remembered at all. I think I got more publicity coming off of that 'Seinfeld' episode than any other thing I did in my career. It was amazing how many people watched that and still talk about that today. But I learned to let it bounce off. At the time, it was a little bit upsetting. I had roots in Seattle and I was having a big year there and when I got over to New York I kind of got lost in the shuffle a little bit. I think I probably would have had my best year ever in baseball had I stayed in Seattle in '88. The way George Argyros, the owner of the Mariners, was doing things in those years, he was trying to unload people if their salaries were getting a little bit too high. He was never fixing what was wrong with that ballclub. He was always getting rid of the guys who were doing well and it wasn't that long afterward that they got rid of Mark Langston and Alvin Davis and cleaned house."

Oh, You Must be Number 21

Ken Phelps' stay in New York, on a personal level, was cloaked in anonymity.

"I got over to New York and there wasn't anybody there other than the players to greet me. After the trade, I never spoke to George Steinbrenner. It wasn't, 'Hey, welcome to the Yankees' or anything like that. I never heard it from him."

It's not as if it cost him anything to say hello.

"I never got any of his money. I never got any Yankee money. I come over there on the last year of a Mariner contract. I played there and then I remember in spring training in '89, I had hit a home run against the Orioles down in Miami that won the game that night. They gave me off the next day. I was in the locker room getting ready to go out to the bench just before the game. Steinbrenner was on the other side of the room with a couple of friends of his. I heard a voice from the other side of the room say, 'Hey, Phelps.' I hadn't spoken to Steinbrenner so I kind of looked that way. I didn't think it was him. Sure enough, it was him. He said, 'Hey, Phelps.' I turn and look at him and he says, 'Looks like you're finally getting your swing.' I said, 'Yeah, yeah, it's coming around, it feels pretty good.'"

And that is all George Steinbrenner ever said to Ken Phelps in the year-and-a-half that he was there. He was traded to the Oakland As and received a World Series ring in 1989, seven years before George Steinbrenner did again.

Brian Doyle

What's a Brian Doyle?

That was the reaction in the Yankee clubhouse when it was learned that Willie Randolph would miss the 1978 postseason with a hamstring injury.

"That's exactly right. I had been up and down seven times that year.

"I was called up the last time when the rosters expanded so I was ineligible for postseason play. The Yankees had to get a special permission from the Commissioner's Office and from the Kansas City Royals, who we were facing in the playoffs, for me to be eligible for the postseason roster.

They gave that permission because of the question everyone was asking: what's a Brian Doyle? I had to go through the same procedure for the World Series and they asked the same question."

Brian Doyle provided the answer: a .423 average, with six hits in the final two games. The 262-point differential between his Series average and lifetime average of .161 is the greatest among players with his number of at-bats in the history of baseball.

Notice? I Don't Need No Stinkin' Notice!

"I did not know that I was going to be playing in the World Series until the day of the first game. I got in the cab to go to Dodger Stadium with Yogi. He said, 'Looks like you're gonna be playing, kid.' That was the first I had heard of it. So I didn't know until just hours before the game."

It's not as if Doyle had time to be nervous . . . because he doesn't get nervous.

"I have never been nervous on a baseball field. What I was more concerned with was keeping my adrenaline down because of the excitement. With the whole family in professional baseball, this could be a once in a lifetime experience. I was excited and just couldn't wait for the chance."

Up and Down and Up and Down and Up and Down and Up and Down and Up and Down and Up and Down and Up and Down

In 1978, Brian Doyle was recalled by the Yankees an astonishing seven different times from Triple-A. The farm club was conveniently located that one season in Tacoma, Washington.

"It was amazing just going back and forth and trying to raise a family having a little son. That was the real pressure. The pressure wasn't the World Series. The pressure was being away from my family and trying to pay bills. And everybody in America understands that type of pressure. So when we got to the World Series, everybody kept on asking, 'Why aren't you nervous?' I'd say, 'I'm not nervous at all' and they'd go, 'Oh yeah, right.' Here's this young kid in a World Series and not nervous. But seriously, I wasn't because of the separation from my family, trying to pay two types of housing bills and meet the monthly bills. That's real pressure when you're flying cross country seven different times and the wife and the son is in limbo. Finally, at the end, I just flew them back to Kentucky with his mother and said, 'Don't move till you hear from me.'"

The overall experience was disconcerting.

"Professionally speaking, it was so difficult, especially for a little guy like myself who was always known as not a lot of pop with the bat but a good contact hitter. To be a good contact hitter and to produce, you have to have continual at-bats."

Which wasn't happening.

"I'd go and sit on the Yankee bench for three weeks at a time and then I'd go back to Triple-A and get some at-bats and then two weeks later I was back doing the same thing in New York again. It was disheartening. Sure, it was great to be in the big leagues and all of them but it was a very difficult situation."

The Yankees saw Doyle as insurance and not a whole lot more than that.

"That's exactly right. They knew that I could catch the ball, throw the ball and turn the double-play and I knew that I could do that with anybody in the game."

A Hairy Comeback

In 1995, Brian Doyle was diagnosed with a rare form of cancer, Hairy Cell Leukemia. Of course, the experience changed his life.

"I have always considered myself strong in my faith. But when something like that happens, reality really, really hits and you find out how strong your faith is. It was just life-changing experience knowing that because of the faith that's in me and the God that I believe in and lives in me that I could go through that."

Doyle had to go through very drastic treatment.

"I was the guinea pig. I was the first person to do double treatments and I did that for almost two years. There was a lot of prayer. One unknown author said, 'Baseball is life with the volume turned up.'

"When the doctor said I was in the final stages of leukemia, it was because of my life in baseball and all of those ups and downs and disheartening consequences."

Here's his message:

"I'm here. When I woke up this morning, I got one day to do something positive for somebody else. That's how it affected me. I got one more day. I don't look at tomorrow like I used to because the moment I live is right now. I remember a good friend of mine saying, 'Use the good china.'"

You're welcome, Brian. Three years later, I was diagnosed with cancer.

With no symptoms and no history of cancer in the family.

January 20, 2002 was the seventh anniversary of Brian Doyle being cancer free.

Bill Skowron

Pay Attention!

If Mariano Rivera completes a force play at second base in the bottom of the ninth inning of the seventh game, chances are the Yankees win the 2001 World Series. Likewise, if Willie McCovey's scorching line-drive with two outs in the bottom of the ninth of the seventh game, is two feet higher and not a bullet to Bobby Richardson, chances are the Giants and not the Yankees win the 1962 World Series.

For the Yankees, it's a damn good thing the ball wasn't hit to Bill Skowron at first base.

"Ralph Houk came out to the mound to talk to Ralph Terry. The Giants had second and third and they were discussing whether or not to pitch to McCovey or to walk him and face Orlando Cepeda with the bases loaded since McCovey's run meant nothing."

During this, Moose was getting sociable with first base umpire Jim Honochick, who later gained fame in the classic Miller Lite commercials.

"They're on the mound talking and I'm talking to Honochick. Houk's back in the dugout and I'm still talking to Honochick when McCovey hits the ball to Bobby

Bill Skowron

Richardson. I couldn't believe it. It was the last out and the game was over."

Get this. Moose doesn't even think he was *looking* at the pitch that Terry threw.

"It was one funny feeling, I'll tell you that."

No Talking!

It's 1966 and Bill Skowron is a year away wrapping up his very substantial career and is playing for his hometown Chicago White Sox.

"Eddie Stanky is the manager. He didn't like the Yankees at all. We had a meeting prior to playing them and he says, "Anybody that gets caught talking to any Yankees, it's gonna cost you $50 bucks. So I'm on first base and Mickey gets a base hit."

Here, it's Mickey who wants to be sociable.

"I'm holding him on first and he says to me, 'How's the wife and kids doing?' I don't say anything. Again, 'How's the wife and kids?' Nothing. 'Moose, I'm talking to you.' I put my glove over my mouth and I say to him, 'I can't talk to you because it will cost me $50 bucks.' And Mickey says, 'All that money I made you in the World Series and I'm not worth $50 dollars?' I never thought he'd come up with something like that. He was a great man."

Robin Ventura

A No-Hitter Like No Other

It was a sunny Sunday in Chicago on July 1, 1990, a getaway game for the Yankees. Greg Hibbard opposed Andy Hawkins. Robin Ventura batted second and played third base. 2:34 later, Hawkins had pitched a no-hitter . . . and lost 4-0.

"I just remember it was a really cold day. It was one of those things where he really shut us down the whole game. I came up later in the game with the bases loaded and two outs and I hit a ball pretty good into leftfield. It was really windy. Jim Leyritz was actually playing left. The ball spun him around a little bit. I figured the way the wind was blowing, it wasn't gonna be a hit. The reaction of the crowd meant something had happened. I found out later the ball hit off his arm or something."

The two-base error cleared the bases to give the White Sox a 3-0 lead.

"It's just a weird thing to sit there on second base, a guy's got a no-hitter and he's losing 3-0."

The outfield follies continued.

"Ivan Calderon actually hit a ball right after that and it was also in the sun. Jesse Barfield got the ball but then dropped it for an error and I scored. It's now 4-0 and the guy still hasn't given up a hit. Just odd things you see in baseball."

Robin Ventura

O-Fer

After spending the 1989 season in Double-A, Robin Ventura skipped Triple-A and made the big club the following year. He started the season on fire, batting .350.

"You really start thinking it's easy."

It ain't. What followed was a slump of slumps of gargantuan proportions, 0-for-41. 16 straight games of nothing. .350 became .117.

"It was a long couple of weeks. For most of it, I didn't even make good contact. I just remember bad things happening."

Like a hit becoming an out.

"In Detroit, I hit a line-drive single to right. It one-hopped the rightfielder and he threw the guy out at second. It wasn't really bad baserunning. It was a hard play for the guy to read so it wasn't really his fault. When you're the hitter, you're thinking, 'Man, this is never gonna end.'"

The slump ended on a sacrifice that the pitcher overran. Ventura was given a hit.

Slammed

On May 20, 1999, playing as the Mets' 115th third baseman in their history against Milwaukee at Shea Stadium, Robin Ventura became the first player in major league history to hit grand slams in both games of a doubleheader. That gave him 15 career slams, the most among active players.

"The grand slams probably first came to my attention after about the eighth one. Once I hit those two in the doubleheader, I think people noticed me hitting grand slams a little bit more."

This good fortune depends on the pitcher.

"I've actually walked a few times with the bases loaded. Those are pitchers that aren't afraid to walk somebody in. That's usually where the game comes down to with the pitcher where they don't want to walk a guy in for a run. They'd rather see if he could hit it."

Ventura says he doesn't get more fired up when he steps in with the bases loaded. He says it's just circumstances.

"Circumstances. You have to be lucky enough to get up that many times in that situation. I've also been fortunate to bat behind some good people that the pitcher obviously didn't want to face. So they took their chances with me and it kind of worked out for me."

The Yankees Then and Now

Times certainly have changed for the opposition coming into Yankee Stadium since Robin Ventura first came on the major league scene in 1990.

"Early on in my career, it wasn't like it is right now. You went in there expecting to win games and if you didn't come out of there with a couple, you were disappointed. Now, I think people go in there trying to get out with one and be on their way."

A Twist of Fate

It was just a routine spring training exhibition home game in Sarasota in 1997.

"It had been raining and they didn't know whether they should call the game or get it in. I was on second base and tried to score on a basehit. I slid into home and my spike got caught in the mud."

The injury was grotesque, shattering his right leg and ankle. Amazingly, Ventura said it didn't hurt. But it hurt to watch. Omar Minaya, the new Expos GM, was a Texas Rangers executive in the stands that day. He compared its gruesome sight with that of Lawrence Taylor snapping Joe Theismann's leg.

"It felt weird. My body just went into shock. There wasn't really any popping or anything like that. That night, they explained the seriousness of it and what they had to do and how long it would take and the possibility I wouldn't play again."

Ventura spent four months on the disabled list during which time he had to learn how to walk again. There was even a question as to whether he would be left with a limp. There have been no problems since.

"I only go into the trainers room now for quality conversation."

Rafael Santana

Robin Ventura is the 69th person to have played for both local teams. He is only the latest player from the left side of the Mets infield to cross the Triborough Bridge and head up the Major Deegan Expressway to his new home.

"It was an honor to play for both teams. When I found out I was going to the Yankees, my heart was in New York. I loved the fans. They appreciated what I did there."

Geographically, it wasn't far

"It was a different atmosphere. Over at Shea Stadium with the Mets, after playing many years with the same guys, it kind of made you feel like you were at home. When I got traded to the Yankees, I went over there and had to meet new people and deal with a different front office. But I was able to make my adjustment and have fun while I was there. So I don't think it was a big deal for me to move from one side to the other one."

Being There

No one highlight or moment resonates inside Rafael Santana's memory bank as a Yankee. Just the totality of the experience at the holy of holies.

"I think the biggest highlight with the Yankees was being able to play at the place where some many superstars and legends played like Ruth, Mantle, Yogi, Mattingly, Winfield and all those guys. So it was thrill for me to be able to play there."

Others come along feeling the same way.

"I was watching the World Series this fall and I saw Mark Grace going to Yankee Stadium for the first time in his life. And it was a thrill for him to b able to walk by all those monuments with Ruth, DiMaggio and those guys. To me, that I had the privilege to play over there and go over behind the wall and see all those great players is something that you will never forget. It's something that you will have in your heart all the time."

5
OUTFIELDERS

Hank Bauer

War is Hell

As we continue to engage in a war different than any other this country has ever waged, no Yankee, past or present, can appreciate it more than Hank Bauer.

One of nine children, he was a child of the Depression. When the Japanese attacked Pearl Harbor, the most unprecedented surprise attack this country experienced until September 11, Bauer enlisted in the Marine Corps.

He was assigned to the Pacific theater and grew into manhood in hells called Guadalcanal, Guam and Okinawa, where his men captured the airfield at considerable cost.

Hank Bauer was one of only six of 64 soldiers who survived the fierce battle. He suffered a shrapnel injury, remnants of which he would play with for the duration of his baseball career.

In his four years of service to our country, Hank Bauer was awarded two Purple Hearts and two bronze stars.

Hank Bauer holds the record for the longest hitting streak in the World Series, 17 games. His Yankees won seven championships in nine years before he was dealt to Kansas City near the end of his career in the deal for Roger Maris.

Having seen hell on Earth, he could identify with another flag-raising: by New York City firefighters at Ground Zero, days after the terrorist attack.

One Subjective Theory

One of Hank Bauer's eight siblings, a brother 3 1/2 years his senior named Herman, "was a better ballplayer than I was."

And he never let Yogi Berra forget it.

"I told Yogi one time, 'You know, Yog, you wouldn't have made a pimple on my brother's ass as a catcher. But you're a hell of a lot better hitter.'"

Herman Bauer never fulfilled his promise as a player. He died at The Battle of Normandy.

Of All the Places to Get Hit

During World War II, Hank Bauer won not one Purple Heart but two.

"I got one on Guam and one in Okinawa. The one on Okinawa was the worst one. I got hit in the left thigh.

"One day we're playing in Yankee Stadium and I think it was Tom Gorman was pitching against us."

Guess where he hit Hank Bauer?

"He hit me right where that damn shrapnel went in and it was stinging. So I got to first base and put my hand on it. Hell, I had a big lump there and I called time. I ran into the dugout and called over our trainer, Gus Mauch. I pulled my pants down and there was a big blood clot there. Casey saw it and said, "Get him the hell out of here. Take him in the training room." Gus put ice on it and it went away right away. It really stung."

Bauer went on the disabled list. Just kidding.

Hank turns 80 in July. "I told my doctor 'I owe my longevity to scotch and cigarettes.' That didn't go over too good."

Jack Clark

'Jack the Ripper' Nervous?

In 1987, playing for the National League champion St. Louis Cardinals, Jack Clark, the main cog in their offensive machine, struck 35 homers, had 106 RBIs and led the league in slugging percentage and walks before an ankle injury ended his season September 9. A contract squabble was all he needed to take his free-agent walk to the Bronx, even though someone with the initials Don Mattingly was ensconced at first.

"To be honest with you, I was a little nervous. For one thing, it was the American League and it was the New York Yankees. You're talking about one of the elite franchises, along with the Celtics and a few other teams, in sports."

He had to re-learn everything, from the umpires to the pitchers to the cities and the ballparks. And there was something else.

"George Steinbrenner could be a little scary because you didn't know what to expect."

Even though he hit .242, his lowest average in a full season, Clark had led the team with 27 homers and escaped The Boss' wrath.

"I'll tell you what, George was great to me. He treated me well and was so gracious. He went out his way to make me feel comfortable and to become a Yankee."

But Clark's heart was left in San Francisco . . . and St. Louis.

"I was one of those guys who should not have switched leagues. But that was because of collusion and a lot of other things that were going on at the time. I was real fortunate to have an opportunity under the circumstances when collusion was going on to get a job anywhere, let alone with the Yankees.

"When George signed me, that kind of opened up the market. George, God bless him, broke through the barrier because he's a man and he wants to win and he wants to win for the City of New York and he wants the best players and he wants to do what this country is based on, having the right to do and say what you want to do. He didn't like not being able to do that. So by bringing me over there, he got in a little bit of trouble but he also stood up for something that was right."

Jack Clark thinks George Steinbrenner doesn't get the credit he deserves.

"People don't understand that, yeah, he's fired a lot of people. But people should tip their hat on what he has been able to do. All he has ever wanted to do is win and bring

World Championships to the greatest city and the greatest organization in baseball and that's New York."

Hanging By a Thread

There is one story from his time with the Yankees that Jack Clark will always remember.

"I've tried to explain to people the character of Billy Martin, what a tough bastard he was. If he was on your side, you couldn't have a better guy.

"We were in Texas and it was about two o'clock in the morning and the kitchen in the hotel caught on fire. I remember the alarms going off and they wanted everybody out of the hotel.

"The hotel was situated right by Six Flags and the water park, so there was a lot of children and families there on vacation.

"They brought everybody downstairs to the lobby so players were down there with shorts on, some with slacks and a T-shirt. People had been sleeping or watching TV. The kids were there in their pajamas and slippers. The players were kind of getting hounded by the kids for autographs."

That's when George Steinbrenner, who happened to be on site, took matters into his own hands.

"He had the players separated for security and had everybody herded into the bar to have privacy."

And then the cab showed up.

"It's two o'clock in the morning and this cab pulls up and it's Billy getting out of the cab. His shirt's all bloody and his ear is just about hanging off of his head. It looked like he had just gotten out of a boxing match. He was all puffy around his face which was contorted. It was so twisted, like there was a big split in his head.

"Billy had a white shirt and tie on, all of which was completely bloody.

"He came in and the kids were screaming. George rushed him into the bar and the trainers told him they needed to get him to a hospital."

That's not what Billy needed.

"He sat down and wanted a drink. He didn't want to go to the hospital until they got him a drink. George put his foot down and said, 'Get him the hell out of here.' That meant guys picking him up if they had to in order to put him in a cab or ambulance or whatever."

Billy eventually left. But there was a ballgame to be played the next night.

"Billy showed up a little bit late, but he came. He got in the jacuzzi, he was all bandaged up, he looked like a mummy. To his credit, he put his uniform on, went out there and took the line-up card with his ear taped back up to the side of his head and his eyes black and blue. He could barely see. I don't know whether we won or lost, but I know we tried the best we could under those circumstances."

Raised Expectations

Before coming to New York, Jack Clark played in two organizations with great histories, the Giants and the Cardinals.

Being with the Yankees, however, was different.

"I never have felt that I wanted to win or try to win or needed to win like here. I mean, the games in spring training were important. That's what I remember, the tradition of the Yankees and how important winning was."

Clark liked what he saw.

"People can talk about it and they can say we want to win. They can say we expect to win. But can they show it on a daily basis with the pride and the tradition to actually walk their talk?

"The Yankees do and George Steinbrenner does, the city does and they have a lot to be proud of. I'm just really fortunate to be able to say that in my career I had an opportunity to wear the pinstripes and be a New York Yankees. I'm very proud of that. I wouldn't want it any other way. They epitomized sport, let alone baseball. It doesn't get any better than that."

There's something about that uni.

"You feel and sense a pride, how you're supposed to carry yourself. It takes over. You have to be pretty tough, pretty strong because there's a lot that's expected. But once you find out how to do it and how to carry yourself and try to fit in there, there's not a better place in sports to be."

In a five-team race, Jack Clark's 1988 Yankees faded at the end of the season, finishing fifth in the East, but only 3 1/2 games behind Boston. He was traded back to the National League to San Diego that winter for pitchers Lance McCullers and Jimmy Jones and outfielder Stanley Jefferson.

Bobby Murcer

Over the Mountain and Through the Woods

Carl Yastrzemski stepped to the plate one afternoon in the old Stadium with 399 career home runs and an inviting short porch in right for his lethal lefthanded stroke. Bobby Murcer was playing center, Ron Woods, acquired for Tom Tresh, was in right.

Murcer picks up the story.

"Yaz hits a line drive to right and the last you see of Woods, he is leaping up and you could see the ball in the glove and he disappears in the stands. There's nobody over there. I'm the only one that got there quick enough. He's knocked out colder than a cucumber."

The glove and the ball are nearby. That's when Murcer went to work.

"I kind of put the glove up towards his hand and put the ball in the glove. The umpire, of course, is running out there, and when he got there, he looked in the stands. He saw the ball in the glove and called him out. They had a pretty big argument. Yaz came all the way out to rightfield to argue that play. If it wasn't for me, he probably would have been there a lot sooner with his 3,000th hit for sure."

Playing the Monuments

Long before there was videotape, there was film. And there is film of Bobby Murcer playing center field in cavernous Yankee Stadium chasing balls bouncing in, around and through the monuments, which stood on the field of play. This was not unlike less accomplished ballplayers chasing Spaldeens underneath parked cars during stickball games in the Bronx as runners circled the bases.

"Not too many balls ever got out to that area. If they did, they were either bouncing or rolling. Not too many were hit in the air. Even though the monuments were on the field, they really didn't come into play as far as them being obstructive to you trying to catch a fly ball.

"It was like 463 feet and that was during the dead-ball era anyway. I chased balls in and around and in the back side of the monuments several times. A couple of times, I actually slid through them to try to cut a ball off that went in one side."

The Prodigal Son Returns

August 6, 1979, the day Thurman Munson was buried in Ohio, was one of the highlights in the career for Bobby Murcer, one of his best friends on the club.

"Billy Martin wasn't going to play me. He said, 'Take the night off. You're tired, you haven't had any sleep in two nights.' I said, 'I feel like I need to play.' And he said, 'Do you want to?' And I said, 'Yes, I really do want to play.' The unusual thing was Billy left me in there late in the game. At that time, they were pinch-hitting me and Lou. He left me in there against Tippy Martinez with the game on the line and that's when I got another base hit, a double down the leftfield line. Who knows why Billy did that?"

Murcer also struck a three-run homer and finished with five RBIs as the Yankees came back from a 5-0 deficit to win 6-5 in yet another unforgettable night inside Yankee Stadium.

Hector Lopez

The 1961 Yankees, immortalized in books and on film, are considered one of the greatest clubs ever . . . with little help from Hector Lopez.

"I didn't have too good a year. I hit .222 with three home runs, something like that. I wasn't playing much. Everyone was hitting home runs. That's one of the worst years I ever had playing baseball."

But in Game Five of the World Series, Lopez drove in five runs in the Yankees' clinching 13-5 victory.

"That made the year for me. I did what I was supposed to."

'Whatta Pair of Hands'

This is what Hector Lopez came to be known as, not a term of endearment.

"I made three errors at third base for Casey one day. Everywhere I went, the ball followed me. The most important thing is, I made the last out of the game. I had the ball hit to me, played it off my chest and threw the guy out at first base."

That was when Dick Young hung the nickname on him.

"'What a pair of hands.' That was my boy, the sportswriter, Dick Young. But he wrote some good stuff about me, though. It didn't move me one way or another. Nineteen fifty-nine was the worst year I ever had fielding. I was a pretty good fielder. That was my forte, fielding the ball, making the plays. That year I didn't do too good and he gave me the business."

Mike Easler

Why Don't Men Ask for Directions?

Mike Easler had just had a wonderful day for the Boston Red Sox. In a spring training exhibition game against the Mets, he had gone 2-for-3 with a home run off Dwight Gooden. This was the 1986 Gooden, purveyor of high octane gas.

"I had just gotten home. It was about 5:30, 6 o'clock. I got a call from Lou Gorman, the General Manager, saying I was traded to the Yankees. Wow! I had stuff spread everywhere in my apartment. I ended up taking off from Winter Haven for Fort Lauderdale. I left about seven or eight that night and ended up in Key West. I drove all night long and got there about seven or eight in the morning."

At ten o'clock, Mike Easler reported for spring training.

"Lou Piniella says, 'How do you feel?' I said, 'I feel great.' He says, 'Can you play right field today?' I'm a DH. I say, 'Sure, whatever.' I hit the ball pretty doggone good."

Sure A World Championship is Nice, But . . .

The player known as the 'Hit Man' was a valued member of the 1979 World Champion 'We Are Familee' Pittsburgh Pirates. But that was before he came to New York to play well for the Yankees.

"It was the greatest experience an athlete can have. I think every ballplayer that plays the game and makes it to the major leagues should play in New York at least one or two years. That's when you reach the top of your profession when you play with one of the New York teams."

The fact that the fans are so demanding fired him up.

"There's the pressure day in and day out, the demands of the fans. The organization is bent on winning, and winning is what it's all about. And when you go there, you can't ever go through the motions. You always have to play at your height. To me, that was the greatest experience of my career in the major leagues.

Even more than Pittsburgh?

"Oh God, yes, it was totally different in New York. You got the media, you got the fans and their love for the game. It's a different love for the game that they have in New York. It's a passion and it's what a true ballplayer should have anyway. You should play with pride and integrity and give everything that you have."

Mickey Rivers

The beloved John Milton Rivers, aka The Gozzlehead, once explained his philosophy of life to a New York writer as follows:

"Ain't no sense worrying about things you have control over, 'cause if you got control over them ain't no sense worrying. And ain't no sense worrying about things you got no control over, 'cause if you got no control over them, ain't no sense worrying about them."

Of course.

The above is official. It was made so in the 1982 Texas Rangers press guide, of which Rivers was a member.

Pushing the Gozzlehead's Buttons So He Can Hear These Magic Words: And They're Off!

It's September, 1978 and the Yankees have just arrived in Boston for an off-the-charts series of importance. The word 'massacre' is not yet on anyone's lips. Jay Johnstone says it's time to assuage the team's sparkplug and his love for horseplay, literally.

"It all started when a bunch of us got together. There was Piniella, Nettles, Jim Spencer, Fred Stanley, myself and one other guy. We got Mickey Rivers in the coffee shop of the Sheraton Boston about 10:30 in the morning before the first game. I lockered next to Mickey and knew him from our days together in the Angels organization."

The Gang of Six gave him a talking to . . . gently.

Mickey Rivers

"We explained to him in order for us to win the division and possibly get to the next level, he needed to get on base. And if he got on base for us as our leadoff hitter and the catalyst for our team, we would probably net about $10,000. And if we netted about $10,000 per man, do you know how many horses you can bet on?"

Mickey's eyes lit up.

"He kept going, '$10,000?' 'Yeah, Mickey, if we win we're getting $10,000. Do you know how much fun you can have at the track?'

"Mickey Rivers was 3-for-3 in the first game before Butch Hobson, the ninth-place hitter for the Sox, came to bat once. He went on to get, I forget exactly how many that series, something like 11 hits. We went on to score about 49 runs on 67 hits or something like that. We beat them four in a row and that's what turned it around."

A gallant comeback that stretched over a 14-game deficit was almost complete.

Ron Kittle

Pay Attention!!

"Everybody's dream is to be a New York Yankee. Everybody's probably told you that."

That from Ron Kittle. He was to be A.L. Rookie of the Year with the Chicago White Sox, soaking up the aura that is Yankee Stadium.

"My first appearance in New York, I was in leftfield while we were taking batting practice. The Thurman Munson video came up on the big screen."

Kittle made the mistake of turning away.

"I was hit with a line-drive smack in the side of the head. And not one time did I flinch or move because I was so engrossed in what I was watching. When you're in an arena like that, you just don't feel any pain. And it was downhill after that."

Attitude Problems

If he had to do it over again, Ron Kittle would have adopted a different attitude when the White Sox traded him to the Yankees.

"I did things the wrong way. I was very upset with the White Sox when I got traded over there. Instead of putting a positive spin on it and saying the New York Yankees needed me to help them out, I wasn't old enough at the time to understand that."

When Kittle did report to the Yankee locker room, he made an unforgettable impression by committing blasphemy.

"Thurman Munson's locker is not used. I walk in and everybody knew I had a sense of humor. I walked over there and threw my gear into Thurman's locker and said, 'Who the hell is this Munson fella?'"

The shrine had been breached.

"Everybody just got real quiet in the locker room."

Retribution

Ron Kittle never imagined home runs would cost him money.

"When I was with the White Sox, I hit a home run against Bob Shirley and another against Tim Stoddard in the same game."

Then Kittle was traded to the Yankees.

"It's about two-and-a-half-weeks later and we have a kangaroo court. I was fined $250 each for hitting home runs against my teammates."

Ron Swoboda

Awed

Time had barely passed between Ron Swoboda's heroics in 1969 with the Mets and arriving as a Yankee in 1971.

"I was gonna tell you this story anyway. I was not prepared to be awed. We had won a World Series with the Mets. It was not that long ago. In 1971, the second half of the season, I got traded from Montreal to the Yankees, which was like getting let out of limbo and back into the real world."

Swoboda remembers the first time he put on the pinstripes.

"I walked through the locker room into the hallway that led you into the home dugout and up those steps. And when I came up those steps all by myself wearing the Yankee pinstripes for the very first time, the first thing you see is the façade that used to be on the old Yankee Stadium and the monuments as you got on to ground level."

Thirty-one years later, the emotions still stir.

"I looked out there and as I'm telling you the story right now, I can feel the little hair on my neck start to stand up. It gave me a chill. It gives me a chill to this day to think about that very first time. I was not prepared to be awed. And I was awed. Everything came in a big rush. It was like me and Babe Ruth, two boys from Baltimore that played for the Yankees. And then the comparison starts breaking down."

And then Ron Swoboda started laughing. Swoboda and Ruth, two guys mentioned in the same breath to this day.

There's Playing in Yankee Stadium and Then There's Playing in Yankee Stadium

Before joining the Yankees, Ron Swoboda played in Yankee Stadium as a member of the Mets in a series of Mayor's Trophy games.

"No big deal. It was an old, dingy other-generation ballpark built in what, 1923?

"But I also played there as an amateur in the Hearst All-Star Game. The Hearst newspaper chain used to sponsor an all-star game with players from all around the United States. Then you'd play the New York all-stars. And I played in that game. I think it was 1961."

Swoboda's performance was, well, let him tell you.

"I was an abysmal failure. There was a pretty good player who played in the game for us named Tony

Conigliaro. He starred in the game and might have been the MVP. He was good. I was scared to death. I was absolutely petrified. I didn't do anything, couldn't get the bat going."

Making an Immediate Impression

Ron Swoboda will never forget the start of George Steinbrenner's stewardship of the Yankees.

"We were in Milwaukee and Ralph Houk didn't know who George Steinbrenner was. I remember he got us all together in the locker room and he says, 'I'm gonna read off some numbers and these are the numbers of guys who need to get a haircut.'"

Swoboda is laughing.

"That was our first encounter with the sensibilities of George Steinbrenner in 1973 when he had taken over the team."

Houk must have loved that.

"There was nothing but sarcasm in Ralph's voice because it was kind of superseding his authority as the manager. It was guys like Bobby Murcer. But George didn't even know their names. You just sent the numbers in."

Swoboda is laughing again. But he stops when he talks about when Houk was let go.

"I remember the words: 'I've been retired.' And he was tearful. Everything he was as a ballplayer was with the Yankees."

Tim Raines

I Went to a Fight and a Baseball Game Broke Out

All hell broke loose inside Yankee Stadium one night in 1998 when Armando Benitez of the Orioles hit Tino Martinez square in the back with a 98 mile-per-hour fastball on the first pitch after he gave up a pivotal home run to Bernie Williams.

"The benches emptied and a big fight broke out. It seemed to go on for an hour. Both benches had cleared and the fight drifted into the Baltimore dugout."

Tim Raines was the next guy up. Benitez was ejected, replaced by Bobby Munoz, the ex-Yankee once billboarded years earlier with so much promise.

"The first pitch I saw, I hit it over the right-centerfield wall. I think that was sort of like payback to the Orioles for them hitting Tino. The crowd just went crazy. I think that moment and that at-bat sticks out more than just about anything I did in New York."

In 21st century baseball where, seemingly, at one time or another, everybody plays with everybody else at one time or another, Bobby Munoz and Tim Raines were teammates in 2001 with the Montreal Expos.

Tim Raines

Billy Sample

Barely a Need to Shower

Billy Sample wore an albatross when he was active, the label of part-time player.

So imagine his excitement when he showed up and found his name in Billy Martin's starting line-up, playing left field, for the 1985 Yankees.

"I was in Baltimore and had singled in a run in my first at-bat. The bases were loaded and I'm up again. Except this time, Ken Griffey Sr. pinch-hit for me."

In the second inning.

"I laugh now when I think about getting pinch-hit for in the second inning but I kind of understood it. It had never happened before. If I had to be pinch-hit for by anybody, I could accept being pinch-hit for by somebody as talented as Ken Griffey Sr., a .296 lifetime hitter. As it turned it, Senior came through with a base-hit."

Sample had heard worse, though.

"Oscar Gamble, when he was with Texas, was already in the batter's box. And he wound up being their leading hitter before that aborted trade to the Yankees in '79. There was a whistle from the dugout and there he was walking back. I guess it can happen to anybody. You certainly would hope that your manager has the decorum and the courtesy and the respect for you to do it as early as possible and not wait until you get in the batter's box."

No HBP

Prior to coming to the Yankees, Billy Sample played half a dozen seasons in Texas, where Billy Martin once managed.

In 1983, Martin was managing the Yankees who were playing a spring training game against the Rangers in Pompano Beach, Florida, a game he was taking way too seriously.

"When I was broadcasting with the Braves and Goose was with the Padres. I wasn't big on talking to the opposing players when I played.

"But I could tell that he wanted to say something to me. We finally met in San Diego under the stands and he asked, 'How did you and Billy Martin get along?' I said, 'Well, he didn't like me, but I didn't dislike him.' I asked him why he would ask. He said that while shagging flies in the outfield before a game, Billy told him to hit me in the head."

Gossage refused to carry out Martin's wishes.

"He said he thought it hurt his relationship with Billy because he didn't do it. He didn't know if Billy was testing him."

Sample knew nothing about it.

"Goose said he could have killed me and I wouldn't have known it. I was so young then, he would have split the helmet, go down to first and not think anything about it."

Roy White

Not 6-4-3 But 48-21-6

One of the favorite trivia questions for Yankee-files to ask is, "What are the three numbers Roy White wore? See above.

"I wore 78 in one of the spring camps early in my career. When I made the club as a rookie in 1966, you didn't ask for a number. The clubhouse man, Pete Sheehy, was in charge of assigning them. He gave me 48."

Soon, White became a regular.

"I was sent out in '67 but returned in '68 and put on 48 again. I was getting in the line-up, playing regularly and having a good year. At the All-Star break, I went to Pete and asked him if I could change the number. I was established a little bit and didn't want such a high number. I looked at what was available and took 21. I wore that for the latter half of '68."

After the season was over, General Manager Lee MacPhail called White into the office.

"He said that next year they were changing my number and they wanted me to wear number six. I said fine."

After White began wearing number six, Pete Sheehy went over to him and let him in on a little secret.

"He told me that was Mickey Mantle's number his rookie season, which I never knew. I was pretty honored because all great Yankees had worn the low numbers."

Overcoming the Scourge

On the all-time Yankee list, Roy White is fifth in games played, seventh in at-bats, ninth in hits and tenth in runs scored. He's in the top-20 in doubles, homers and RBIs.

Not bad for a kid stricken with polio.

"My memories of it are pretty vague. My grandmother was working in a hospital as a nurse's aide or something and she told my mom to call an ambulance. Polio was really going around a lot then and that's what I was diagnosed with. An ambulance came out and took me to the hospital."

White remembers being there a long time, as long as a month or two, getting shots regularly and spinal taps.

"I remember when I came back to school, they put me back a grade. Everybody had passed me. But then the next year, they moved me back. I guess the fact that they caught it early and my grandmother got me to a hospital and they were giving me penicillin worked. I was never affected by paralysis. I was lucky."

Rondell White

Rondell White grew up in rural Gray, Georgia, population 2,000, about 90 miles from Atlanta. It is hardly a sprawling metropolis.

"We had one red light. Now we've got three."

Rondell White

White was a vital cog in the Jones County High School team that won the state championship. White batted third, two spots behind leadoff hitter Willie Greene, who came to the majors with Cincinnati before drifting off to Baltimore, Toronto and the Cubs.

Floyd White, Rondell's father, is an avid baseball fan who was a faithful viewer of the old "Game of the Week" on NBC.

As a free agent last winter, the front-runners for White were Seattle, the Yankees and the Cubs, who hoped to retain his services.

"Once the Yankees were in it, there was no other place I was going to go."

That made dad smile.

The Fall Classic

The World Series was played despite World Wars I and II, Korea and Vietnam, a depression and countless other cataclysmic events in our history. All except 1994.

That was Rondell White's rookie season with Montreal. When the players walked out after the games of August 11, Felipe Alou's Expos had a 74-40 record, by far the best in the National League. They were six games better than Atlanta, eight games better than Cincinnati, which led the Central, and 16 games on top of Los Angeles in the West.

Ken Hill, already 16-5, was Montreal's ace. Right behind him was Pedro Martinez at 11-5, a pitcher whose best days lay ahead of him. The closer was John Wettleland, who, after play resumed the following April, was the Yankee closer.

The outfield featured Larry Walker, a .332 hitter who was to move on to Colorado, Moises Alou, who hit .339, and Marquis Grissom. No wonder White was the fourth outfielder.

When they packed away the bats and balls, the Yankees had a 70-43 record, best in the American League, 6 1/2 games ahead in the East over Baltimore, three games better than Central-leading Chicago and 18 1/2 games ahead of Texas which led the West with a 52-62 record. Really.

Starting August 12, the leagues were forced to cancel their games on a day-to-day basis. The strike marked the eighth work stoppage in 23 seasons and the fifth players strike in history.

On September 14, Acting Commissioner Bud Selig cancelled the remainder of the 1994 season including the Divisional Series, the League Championship Series and the World Series, the first time that happened in 90 years.

Rondell White hopes his first season as a Yankee ends in a belated Series appearance in October.

Ever So Close

Rondell White witnessed the magic firsthand.

After Tino Martinez' dramatic home run in the ninth inning of Game 3 of the 2001 World Series, Rondell White was in Yankee Stadium for Games 4 and 5.

He was there with Clifford Floyd of the Florida Marlins. Together, not so long ago, they had come through the fertile Montreal farm system and were young stars in the Expos outfield.

In Game 4, White and Floyd saw Scott Brosius incredibly replicate Martinez' feat in the ninth and Derek Jeter's home run win it in the tenth.

Then, Alfonso Soriano won Game 5 with a single to right in the 12th inning. They may have been the three most dramatic World Series games ever played in succession.

"It was unbelievable, the fans talking baseball on every pitch," said White. "There's nothing else like it. It gave me goosebumps."

When the World Series is played in 2002, it is his fervent hope he will not need a ticket.

Johnny Callison

"I had such a hard time with the Cubs, but it was a surprise to come to the Yankees. I was happy to go over there because Ralph Houk was such a helluva guy and I enjoyed playing for him. He made me feel comfortable."

Callison said that first year was scary.

"I come from Bakersfield, a little town in California. You always hear about Yankee Stadium. It overwhelms you. But then you get on the field and it's another ballfield. But it's impressive."

Callison and his family never moved to New York, remaining in the Philadelphia area where he had made a name for himself years before.

"I live right off the Turnpike here and I commuted back and forth because I wasn't playing every day. You're close enough and yet you're not close enough. I didn't want to live in New York, I knew that."

Callison says the commute was tough.

"It was 100 miles door-to-door. I had my GTO running up and down that Turnpike. I could make it in an hour and a half at night, an hour, forty minutes daytime. I only got two tickets. That Turnpike, they sneak up on you."

Drive it every day and you get to know where the speed traps are.

"I figured that out after I got a couple of tickets."

The Yellow Rose of the Bronx?

Johnny Callison's most famous swing came in New York City, across town at Shea Stadium when his three-run home run in the bottom of the ninth off Dick Radatz won the 1964 All-Star Game for the National League. But something that happened to him as a Yankee touched him even more.

"In '72, we had a pretty decent team. We were right in it until the last week or so. CBS owned the club then. I'll never forget, one night I hit a double to knock in the winning run and they sent my wife a dozen yellow roses, which I never heard of. That impressed the hell out of me. Of course, Steinbrenner got there and he got rid of all us old guys."

Tom Tresh

How Many Times Does it Happen That the Guy Who Makes the Great Catch Usually Leads Off

Or so it seems. In 1967, with the score tied 6-6 in the top of the ninth at the Stadium, Danny Cater of the White

Sox, a future Yankee who was the swag for Sparky Lyle, hit a drive to deep left field.

"I dove into the stands and caught it and robbed him of a home run. It was really a neat thrill because when you make a great play, the fans are standing and cheering me and you run all the way back in with the third out into the dugout and the fans are still cheering. Well, I happened to be the leadoff hitter."

When Tresh stepped outside of the dugout, the fans started cheering again.

"It was a constant noise directed at you and what a thrill! I got up the plate and hit the ball out of the park to win it."

And the crowd kept cheering.

Checking the Outfield Defense, It's Tom Tresh in Left, Mickey Mantle in Center and Roger Maris in Right

Imagine being Tresh.

With the military claiming the playing services of Tony Kubek for most of the 1962 season, Tom Tresh played short-stop well enough for the Yankees to eventually be named the American League Rookie of the Year. Kubek returned later that season and Tresh moved to the outfield.

"Ralph Houk called me in the office in Minneapolis in late August or early September and said that Tony was back. "You played really well and we need both of you guys in the office. Tony and Bobby played a long time together. You've done a great job filling that position and if you want to stay at shortstop, that's fine."

But Houk said he had an idea.

"He said, 'I'd like to put together an outfield of Roger Maris, Mickey Mantle and Tom Tresh.' Of course, that had a little bit of a ring to it, especially when your idol is Mickey Mantle. Ralph said left field would not be a platoon position anymore. If you go out there and want to do that, it's your position. You don't have to try out for it, I'm not gonna take you out of it, it's yours. You've proved you can hit and done very well for us defensively. A shortstop has all the tools to play the outfield."

There was just one tiny problem.

"I think the last time I had been in the outfield was junior high school.

"But a shortstop's position where you have to go back on the ball a lot, you're in on all the throws, you're in on the longer relays, your arm has to be pretty good. So if you can play shortstop, you really have the tools probably to play the outfield. Left field at the Stadium was unique because it was a short left field line. A lot of balls would be hit down that line and would bounce off the fence or the wall and into fair territory. Because of my shortstop background, I had a lot of success throwing guys out at second base. Throwing from left field to second base was very much like going in the hole at shortstop and throwing to first base. Same technique instead of throwing the ball in the air, it went in one hop. I had good success at it."

6
SUPERSTARS

Don Mattingly

Listen to Mike Easler talk about his time with Don Mattingly.

"He epitomized that passion and desire for the game. I was there in '87 when he had seven consecutive games with home runs. I'm telling you, Donnie Mattingly was my hero. As a matter of fact, I came over with the nickname 'The Hit Man' and when I left his nickname was 'The Hit Man.' He took it. Shame on him. But that's New York for you."

Showdown

One of the highlights of Ron Kittle's stay with the Yankees was watching Don Mattingly and Wade Boggs wage a battle for the batting title on the final day of the season in Boston.

"Donnie had to go 5-for-5. I think he went 4-for-5 and his last at-bat was a line drive to shortstop that Eddie Romero caught. Wade Boggs sat out the game and he's on the big screen smiling and nodding his head. All of a sudden, you see him putting on his batting gloves because if

Donnie gets a hit, he would have had to bat the next inning to win the title. Just seeing all that stuff going on was pretty remarkable."

There's a story inside that story.

"I'm hitting behind Donnie that day and he broke a bat. I grabbed the bat and I just yelled up to the stands, '100 bucks for a Mattingly bat.' Sure enough, some guy whips out a $100 bill. Lou Piniella is managing and he says, "Only Ronnie Kittle could do that."

Jason Giambi

The Wooing Was Alluring

Within days of their heartbreaking World Series defeat at the hands of the Arizona Diamondbacks, the Yankees began in earnest their wooing of Jason Giambi.

The 2000 American League MVP and runner-up to Ichiro Suzuki in 2001 received phone calls from Manager Joe Torre, Roger Clemens and Derek Jeter. Also recruited to sell him on the program was then-Mayor Rudy Giuliani who implored him to switch coasts because the Yankees were in need of another Italian star in the tradition of DiMaggio, Lazzeri, Crosetti, Berra and Rizzuto.

Jason Giambi

"Pop, It's Not Number 7, But We Got the Pinstripes"

So spoke Jason Giambi at his introductory press conference with the New York media.

Then he cried.

His father, John, a bank president in a town 30 miles from Los Angeles, grew up idolizing the Yankees in general and Mickey Mantle and Yogi Berra in particular. He was a catcher with dreams of his own until a knee injury ended his baseball career in junior college.

So John did the next best thing. He passed that adoration on to his sons, Jason and Jeremy. As a reminder, Jason wore uniform number seven all his life until he signed with the A's as their second-round draft choice in 1992. There, Scott Brosius, soon to become a Yankee, had it. So he chose No. 16, the numerals adding to 7. In New York, it's No. 25, same reasoning.

"I'm just a normal kid off the street who had a dream to make this happen," Giambi said.

Part of that dream involves jewelry.

"I want to get a few of those things that Yogi uses for toe rings."

What else do you do with 10 World Series rings?

Missing the Mick

Years ago as a kid with the San Diego Padres, shortstop Ozzie Guillen got out of going to Instructional League by telling the ballclub his mother had died in Venezuela.

When he got there, his mother told him never to do that again.

In 1992, Jason Giambi, fresh off the U.S. Olympic Team in Barcelona, did heed the call of the A's and reported to Instructional League.

At the same time, his father and younger brother, Jeremy, traveled to an autograph show at the Pomona Fairgrounds in California to meet their idol, Mickey Mantle.

The Mick got out from behind the table he was sitting at to pose for pictures with the Giambis. People waiting in line behind them were getting antsy. Jason had missed the show.

Mickey Mantle died from liver cancer on August 13, 1995. Jason Giambi, in his rookie season, hit home runs each of the next three days.

Porch Power

Jason Giambi received a seven-year contract worth $120 million dollars. Not bad for a former 43rd round draft choice of the Milwaukee Brewers in 1989.

"I couldn't fathom all of the money that I had before," he said. "To have this situation is mind-boggling."

He did have one other request.

When asked about the possibility of Yankee Stadium aiding and abetting the lefthanded pull-hitter's ability to strike 50 homers, he said, "I'm not going to put that pressure on myself, but I was trying to get them to make it about 290 down the right-field line. I was trying to work with the dimensions."

Giambi on Broadway

At the Ed Sullivan Theater on Broadway, Jason Giambi visited the Late Show with David Letterman the day he signed.

With permission granted by Worldwide Pants Inc., from the home office in Wahoo, Nebraska, here are his top 10 reasons for wanting to play for the New York Yankees:

10. I want to help the team fight the embarrassment of not winning a world championship in 14 months.

9. When you say, "David Wells sent me," you get half-price drinks at Hooters.

8. Pinstripes are slimming.

7. After Chuck Knoblauch, people will think I have a great arm.

6. I hear Steinbrenner is a dream to work for.

5. Miss Cleo told me.

4. Diving into the stands for a foul ball and "accidentally" landing on Donald Trump's date.

3. Have you ever been to Oakland?

2. In New York, I'm closer to my favorite talk show host—Regis. And the number-one reason for wanting to play for the New York Yankees . . .

1. After the game, cruising bars with Giuliani and picking fights.

7
SUPERSUBS

Ross Moschitto

Mickey's Caddie

They are a small group of players, players who spelled The Mick in centerfield in the late innings in spacious Yankee Stadium.

The last is remembered best, Ross Moschitto, number 53.

Despite what major league records say, he could hit. He hit so well at Johnson City in the Appalachian Rookie League in 1964 that he was named the Player of the Year.

In 1965, he made the spectacular leap from Class-A to the Bronx, just in time to be part of the beginning of the end after five straight appearances in the World Series.

"I felt almost like I was a jinx. That's one reason why I signed with the New York Yankees. I had other offers from St. Louis and the Mets. The Yankees were a championship team. I get there and they're at the bottom of the heap."

In a 110-game career, he batted just 36 times. One of those was a home run.

"It was one of those real laughers. We were losing something like 15-2. We had just come off a roadtrip from LA where I actually went 2-for-2. So that game I got in early. Mickey had hit a home run earlier."

Moschitto was facing Jim Perry, Gaylord's older brother.

"He threw me a slider inside and I swung at it and missed. Then he got one up and in and I creamed it to leftfield."

The papers jumped on the story.

"They were saying 'The Next DiMaggio' and that I was hitting them where Joe D hit them and all this nonsense."

His parents still have the ball at their home in California.

Jay Johnstone

Jay Johnstone received a World Series ring with the 1978 Yankees. But he would never, ever confuse their collective personality with the champions next year, the 'We Are Familee' Pittsburgh Pirates.

"That was a team that went against the grain in what you'd want in a team as far as relationships go. The '78 team was a bunch of individuals. There were a lot of cliques on that team. A lot of guys would spar back and forth and you sometimes didn't know if it was for fun or if it was for real. There were a lot of guys on that team that didn't like each other. I swear if the game were to end and you would be walking across the street and somebody got hit by a bus, most of the guys would keep going and leave you there. But once they put on the Yankee uniform and walked across the white line, it was a whole different group of guys. For whatever it was on that field, when they put on the uniform that said 'Yankees', they came together. As soon as they went on the other side of the line and got into the clubhouse, they went back to being themselves again. I've never seen anything like it in my whole life."

Payback

Jay Johnstone played sparingly for the Yankees in 1979 before being dealt on the old June 15 deadline in the big Dave Wehrmeister trade. He played out his option that season with the Pods and signed with the Dodgers. That set the stage for a pivotal at-bat against the Yankees in the 1981 World Series.

The Dodgers lost the first two games in New York. In Game Three on Friday night, Fernando Valenzuela staggered to victory, allowing 17 baserunners. The following afternoon, the Dodgers trailed 6-4 when Johnstone pinch-hit in the sixth inning.

Here is Jay Johnstone as Babe Ruth in 1932 at Wrigley Field.

"The irony of it is I had predicted it and showed the writers in batting practice if I got into the game today this is what I was going to do: hit a home run. They said, 'Yeah, right.'"

Johnstone told an audience of about 20 writers how he was going to do it.

"I said, 'Here's what I'm gonna do. I'm gonna shorten up my stance just a little bit and shorten my stride. Instead of taking my normal six-inch stride, I'm gonna go up and down real fast so I can get that bat head out and be quick.' Then I proceeded to hit, like, five or six balls out of the ballpark in batting practice. Then I told them, 'If Gossage comes in and throws me a fastball, it's gonna be up in the strike zone, I'm gonna raise my hands a little bit so my hands are shoulder high.' And they're still going, 'Yeah, right, right.'"

Everyone was now on notice.

"I got in the game early, in the sixth inning, and Ron Davis was pitching. But he threw the ball just as hard as Gossage. He threw me that fastball right out over the plate and I did exactly as I said."

The homer tied the game 6-6 and the Dodgers eventually won. The writers came down after the game.

"They couldn't believe it. Of course, I know it's one of those things where the chances of me doing that were slim and none. I got the opportunity and it just happened to work out my way and I became the hero for that."

Gil McDougald

I Can Hear Clearly Now

Just the very act of calling Gil McDougald, the 1951 American League Rookie of the Year, for a phone interview for this book could be filed under the term 'miracle.'

McDougald had gradually gone deaf in both ears after a freak accident in which he was hit above the right ear by a line drive during batting practice in 1955.

A cochlear implant behind his right ear changed everything.

"It's funny. When you've been deaf for 15 years and then all of a sudden, things change."

Turns out a newspaper column in the *New York Times* that described McDougald's plight was read by a doctor in Washington D.C..

"He picked it up and he happened to be a Yankee fan. He called my wife right away. I don't even think it was 9 o'clock in the morning and he already had set up the appointment. What happens is you find out when you're entirely deaf that it is a hearing world. And if you can't communicate, it is really difficult."

Gil McDougald can now hear the joy and squeals of delight from his 11 grandchildren.

Something That May Never Happen Again

It's one thing to switch positions twice. It's quite something else to play all three positions, second, short and third, with such distinction as to make the All-Star team at each spot.

But that's exactly what Gil McDougald accomplished in the 50s, something no one has done since.

"I think anybody can play the three positions. But there's no way you can play three positions constantly and do the job you'd like to do. If you stayed at one position, you gotta be better because you get more used to the position and don't have to make adjustments every day."

Johnny Blanchard

You Want Anchovies With That?

It's 1955 and Johnny Blanchard has just completed his Eastern League season in Binghamton, New York, where he won the home run and RBI crowns. He was heading home, or so he thought.

"The last game of the season, the wife and I had packed up the car and we were all ready to drive back to Minnesota. After the last game, the whole club went up to a little pizza parlor for some pizza and a couple of beers."

About midnight, the phone rang in the pizza parlor. The caller asked for Johnny Blanchard.

"Some guy's on the line saying he's George Weiss. I didn't know it. He says, 'Blanch, we want you to report tomorrow morning to Yankee Stadium. Well I told the guy, 'Yeah, yeah. Have another beer, pal,' and I hung up the phone."

Blanchard started back to the table and the phone rang again. Of course, it was for him.

"The guy said to me, 'Don't you hang up again. This is George Weiss. You be here tomorrow by noon.' And it was really George Weiss."

The Blanchards drove all night to the Bronx, "an adventure and a half," and checked into the hotel at 10 a.m. He was at the Stadium at noon.

It's Not Just a Job, It's An Adventure

When he wasn't spelling Yogi Berra or Elston Howard behind the plate, Johnny Blanchard found playing time in the outfield.

"We were playing a ballgame in 1961 one evening in Cleveland and Houk put me in right field. Of course, I was no gazelle out there. Bobby Richardson was playing second base.

"In the old Cleveland ballpark, there was an opening in the stands through which the sun would shine. At about 8 or 8:10 at night, it would hit the right-fielder dead in his eyes, just above the hitter."

Blanchard would put the bill of his cap down and his hand up to block the sun. But he was also blocking the hitter out.

"For about eight minutes there was no way until that sun dips down that you can see."

It's eight minutes of hell.

"Especially for a guy like me. I was no Mickey Mantle in the outfield, I was no Hank Bauer by any means."

Willie Kirkland, the Indians outfielder, stepped to the plate. You know what's coming next.

"I saw him take a swing. I know he swung at the ball by his feet, by his legs and all. But I didn't have a clue where the ball went. Right away, I looked at Richardson at second base. Bobby kept pointing to the foul line. I kept drifting over toward the area of the pole. I looked back at him and he kept pointing like it was a foul ball."

Blanchard is looking up trying to pick the ball up and starts banging his glove.

"I get over to the stands and the people are howling. One guy yells out at me, 'Hey, dummy, the ball is in right-center out of the park.' I looked down at Bobby and he was facing me and had his hands on his knees. I could see his shoulders were just jiggling he was laughing so hard he couldn't pick his head up. As soon as the ball was hit, Bobby knew it was out of the park. I'm in the corner dancing around, looking for the ball, just hoping it doesn't hit me in the head."

"Richardson says, 'Blanch, I had to give it to you. I know you didn't see it. I knew it was gone.'"

That's the last time Johnny Blanchard took direction from Bobby Richardson.

Dave Bergman

A Deceiving O-Fer

In his first call-up to the show at the end of the 1975 season after winning the Double-A Eastern League batting title, Dave Bergman went 0-for-17. He only struck out four times.

"I have to tell you, between you, me and the fence-post, I certainly didn't swing the bat all that well. But there were about four particular plays, two on bunts and two that were hit up the middle that I, in my own mind, thought not only I was safe, I was safe by at least a step."

Back in those days, unless it was a clean hit, a rookie was banged out.

"I was a little disenchanted with the results. However, in retrospect, it was a great learning experience. I thought I could have just as easily been 4-for-17 or even 5-for-17."

His last game was against Jim Palmer.

"I went 0-for-4 but hit the ball right on the screws twice. Of the 17 at-bats, I felt like I had eight good at-bats and nine terrible at-bats."

Preparing for the Future

Dave Bergman was one of those rare players who did not embark upon his professional career until he graduated from college. In this case, from Illinois State University armed with a business administration degree and a focus in finance. Seventeen seasons and 1,349 games and one great pension later, he entered the business arena managing other players money. *While* he was playing, not after.

"I went to school and worked every off-season. I'm a firm believer that athletes, if they're gonna waste their time, they need to waste their time in the off-season trying to figure out what they want to do when their career is over. The reason is that most athletes, after their career is over, spend five, six, seven years floundering, trying to find a profession that is acclimated for their intelligence, or something they really like to do."

Bergman had a different theory when it came to himself.

"I felt 'why don't I do that while I'm playing and when I'm done, I'm ready to roll n' roll in the field I know I want to pursue.'"

Bergman's potential clients were right there in the locker room with him.

"My first professional client was Alan Trammell. At that time, I was helping him invest his money. I was not personally investing his money. He had somebody else doing it. When I retired, he called me and said he wanted to be my first professional client."

Bergman prides himself in knowing the field, actually, two of them, baseball and business.

"One of the things that helps me in the business that I'm in is these guys can't trick me. I know all their tricks. I know when they sleep, I know when they eat, I know how they think. In many cases, I can think five years ahead for them because I know some of the issues that are gonna take place in their professional career."

Which makes him invaluable.

Phil Linz

Maestro, If You Please, Do You Know 'Play Me or Keep Me?'

It was a variation on a popular theme.

"I said it to Ralph Houk. It broke up the bus. I'm glad he got a kick out of it. Joe Garagiola was announcing for us at the time and he came up with the idea. We were in the back of the bus as usual, cutting up, making jokes. I guess I got 4-for-5 one day. I was hot. I was getting two hits, three hits, four hits. As soon as I went 0-for-3, I was right back on

Phil Linz

the bench. Of course, they kept me. They didn't play me. That was the worst part."

Mr. Laffs

No listing of every hot nightspot in Manhattan over the last 40 years would be complete without this one.

"We lived at the Loews Midtown on 48th and 8th Avenue. I was living there with Bud Daley, a lefthanded junkball pitcher. I had a '64 T-Bird. They let us stay there for $7 a day. We had lived in the Bronx where we were paying $6 a day. Bob Tisch set us up, told us to come downtown for a dollar more a day. We had a swimming pool and free parking for the T-Bird. Around three o'clock, we'd drive up 8th Avenue and go to the St. Moritz, double park and then go up and see Mickey. We'd wait for him to get ready and then we'd go through Central Park to go to the ballpark."

Then came the fateful elevator ride.

"I meet this stewardess and get her number. We're going up to Boston for a weekend series. When we get back, I give her a call. She lives at 65th Street and First Avenue. We're in a cab and she says, "You know, there's no guys in this building. There's nothing but girls, all airline stewardesses. There's like about 50 guys and 300 stewardesses." The next day, we saw the superintendent of her building and signed a lease for an apartment."

Think that's lucky? Get this.

"Bob Anderson was my next door neighbor. He played left halfback at West Point and then for the Giants. He had just gotten out of football after hurting his knee. The superintendent asked if we wanted to become partners and would be interested in opening up a club inside an empty store on

First Avenue. Why not? We'll have some fun and do it for laughs."

Ralph Houk didn't think it was so funny.

"He called me in the office during the season and said, 'I hear you're opening a place. We don't think it's a good idea.' I said, 'Why not?'

"He says, 'Well, you're playing here in New York and it's gonna distract you from playing.' I said, 'Well it's too late now. I already have my money into it.'"

Right before the club opening in December, 1965, Phil Linz was traded to Philadelphia for Ruben Amaro.

"I'm pretty sure that was one of the reasons. Of course, I only hit .207 that season. I was just pretty lucky it was close."

Here, Catch

Phil Linz, a native of Baltimore, invites his parents to Memorial Stadium to see him play for the Yankees. He will never, ever forget this.

"It is June 4, 1963, and I'm at bat. I hit a foul ball into the stands. My father catches it."

This made the Baltimore papers.

"My father sends a postcard to that show in New York 'I've Got a Secret.' Three weeks later, around World Series time, my parents come up from Baltimore. They put them up in a hotel and put them on the show. The celebrities guessed it."

Not Doing it For the Money

Phil Linz was out of baseball at 29.

"I was pretty bored. I wasn't making any money either, so that was another reason. After the 1964 season and the harmonica thing, the Yankees sent me a contract for $20,200. The $200 was for music lessons. That was in my contract. Actually, they were repaying my fine that I got that summer. I got fined $250 by Yogi."

Time for trivia. Can you imagine who was the youngest ex-player ever invited to Old Timers Day at Yankee Stadium?

"It was a record. I wasn't shocked, I was embarrassed big time. I was too embarrassed to go. I never showed up there, no way, no way. I was younger than most of the players on the current team. I didn't go back for years."

This is Easy

Phil Linz was 1-for-3 in the 1963 World Series against the Dodgers. The '1' was against Koufax. Of course.

"It was my first time at bat. First pitch fastball hit one bounce between third and short that went through. It looked to me like he was so easy to hit."

Oh, you're the guy.

"He didn't have any deception and came right over the top. The ball was nice and white and came right out of his hand. It looked so easy.

"I was a good fastball hitter, a good high fastball hitter. I threw the bat head out and it went through the infield."

Time to hit again.

"The next time at bat, he threw me some fastballs that I could hardly see. It was like jet propulsion. It looked the same to me. The ball was released out of his hand and I saw it real well. Here it comes and then it would just explode and blew right past me. It's hard to get your hands started. Incredible."

8
MANAGERS AND COACHES

Bobby Cox

The unheralded Bobby Cox, who has won with all different types of teams in Atlanta, will forever hold the Yankees close to his heart. For it all started for him in pin-stripes.

Cox left eight long years in the minors behind him when he was acquired by the Yankees, along with fellow third baseman, Mike Ferraro, in the winter of 1967.

The following spring, Manager Ralph Houk had them do battle. Cox scuffled, while Ferraro was on fire and won the job.

As the team flew home to New York, someone showed Mickey Mantle the stat sheet. Ferraro had batted about .353, about four points higher than Mantle.

Mickey yelled out, "Hey, Mike, you led the club in hitting." Ferraro yelled back, "Who'd you expect?"

But it was Cox who started on Opening Day. It might as well have been yesterday.

"It was against the Detroit Tigers. I can remember the pitcher was Joe Sparma and I can remember the national anthem in the old Yankee Stadium before they refurbished it. I was at attention saluting the flag during the anthem. I went up on my tippy-toes to stretch a little bit and I got some cramps in the back of my legs. I got a basehit off Sparma, I hit a line-drive off him. The old tradition in Yankee Stadium, packed house on Opening Day. Babe Ruth, Gehrig and Mantle and all those people."

'68 was to be Mantle's final season, parked at first base, taking throws from Bobby Cox.

"You know, I'm in the Hall of Fame as well as Mickey because I was involved in a triple play with him. The bases were loaded and Dooley Womack was pitching. Someone hit a line-drive to him, he threw to me at third and I threw back to Mickey and we got a triple play. The ball got to the Hall of Fame. So I can say I'm in Cooperstown with the Mick."

Frank Howard

In the opening game of the 1963 World Series, playing in the old Yankee Stadium with the field dimensions that stretched northward to Yonkers, 6-7, 275-pound Frank Howard of the Los Angeles Dodgers batted against Whitey Ford.

"I hit a line-drive off the monuments. For most guys, it would be a stand-up triple or possible inside-the-park homerun. For me, it was a head-first slide just to get a double out of it."

Legend has it that Tony Kubek, playing shortstop, jumped for the ball.

"I didn't see him jump for it. You know, in World Series play, you're psychologically so high, especially in the first game. I knew it had a chance to go in the gap for extra bases."

It makes for a better story that Howard never saw if Kubek jumped.

Hondo and Mickey

"You know, it's kind of a funny thing in our business. As we get a little bit older and look back on our careers, our minds expand. The balls keep going further and going there more often."

Frank said he talked to Mickey Mantle right before he passed away.

"He asked me a question: 'How many times did you strike out?' And I said, 'About fourteen hundred and something.'

"He said, 'Well, I got you beat. It's about seventeen hundred. How many times did you walk?'

"I said, 'Probably about fifteen hundred times.' He said, 'I got you beat, about eighteen hundred times.'

"He says, 'That's about 6,000 at-bats. Do you realize that based on a 600 at-bat year for 10 years, we didn't do much on a baseball field?' That put it in its proper prospective."

Welcome to Baseball's Golden Age

Frank Howard says he doesn't want to detract from the "great things these young people are doing today.

"I've seen Stargell, I've seen McCovey, I've seen Frankie Robinson, I've seen Killebrew. I've seen guys hit baseballs unbelievable distances. But you get the mighty McGwire. He has consistently hit the ball further than anybody that's ever played this game, including Ruth."

Howard asked Killebrew if he ever hit 50 home runs in a season.

"Harmon told me, 'No, Frank, I hit 49 twice.' I said, 'Can you imagine a guy hitting 70 or more home runs?' He said, 'Not in my wildest dreams.'

"That's 21 home runs more than one of the greatest power hitters and Hall of Famers that ever lived.

"People say to me, 'Well, the ball's juiced, the pitching's thinner, the ballparks are small.' Today's guys with that size and that strength are making them play smaller.

"I don't care. You hit 70 or 73 home runs, that has got to be recognized. To sit back and say, 'That's the way it used to be,' that's a bunch of bull. They talk about the good old days. Well, the good old days are today."

He Might Have Won the Player of the Week Award

Playing for Washington in 1968, over the course of just one week, Frank Howard struck 10 home runs. In just 20 at-bats.

"Those 10 home runs were hit off of Detroit, Boston, Cleveland and then Detroit."

Retaliation was never on order.

"I thought after a while someone might crease me, but it never happened."

Frank says this major league record is no big deal.

"If you can't hit 10 home runs in a week, you shouldn't be playing in that league.

"Somebody once asked me, 'Did you really hit a ball over the left field roof at Tiger Stadium?'

"I said, 'If you can't hit one over that roof, you shouldn't be playing in this league.'

And then Frank Howard added, "That's why they call it the big leagues. The thrill of competing against the world's greatest baseball players, I don't think there's anything that beats it."

Buck Showalter

The First Day of School

Buck Showalter remains surprised at the opposition for his first regular season game as manager of the Yankees.

"We beat the Red Sox, which I thought was pretty strange. With the troubles we were having drawing back then, I know it sounds crazy to say now, to play the Red Sox on Opening Day—a day you could play the Little Sisters of the Poor and fill the house up. I remember a pop up by Jody Reed to end the game. Steve Farr was pitching. I didn't think it would ever come down and thought it was foul. Charlie Hayes squeezed it, and I started thinking about my dad."

Buck Showalter's father, William Nathaniel II, died two weeks after he got the Yankee job. His son, William Nathaniel IV, was born a month later.

Get in the Car, We're Taking a Trip Downtown to Headquarters

Will any major league manager ever have a day more unusual than the one Buck Showalter had in 1992 when he was summoned before Commissioner Fay Vincent in the late morning before a day game?

"Fay Vincent called the house looking for me. My wife, Angela, told him it's a day game following a night game so he spends the night at the Stadium on a cot. So I get a call from the Commissioner's secretary shortly after my wife called to tell me what happened. I was told that 'the Commissioner had a problem with your testimony yesterday in the Steve Howe case and he would like to see you' at 11 or 12 o'clock sharp, I forget which. We had a game at one o'clock."

The Commissioner didn't care. Enter General Manager Gene Michael.

"He basically told Stick he was gonna be there for both of us and to worry about the game later. It was a pretty tough ride down there."

Then Showalter disappeared behind closed doors.

"I went in and told the truth. He had a problem with our testimony. He thought it contradicted the Commissioner's drug program. I can remember Fay Vincent smoking a cigar and having four or five of his people around him. The one thing I remember most was Jack Lawn."

Lawn was listed by the Yankees as Vice President, Chief of Operations.

"He was a pretty cool customer. He had been in the D.E.A. with the Bush Administration. I was the first one in and the first one out. He said, 'What happened?' I told him I was told that I had effectively resigned from baseball. Jack was reading a paper. He looked back down and said, 'Ah, he's bluffing, don't worry about it.' Jack went in and was told something like he should have checked his sense of ethics and morals at the door and done what's best for this Commissioner's Office."

That's when Jack Lawn pulled out a card and started writing.

"One of the security guys or henchmen or whatever, said to him, 'What are you doing?' He said, 'I just want to make sure I get that right. You've got to understand that I was in the Marines for 12 years. We were taught to never abandon our wounded and leave them on the battlefield. And that's the way we feel about Steve Howe.'"

The process left Showalter introspective.

"The question I had to ask myself was 'would I be down here on Steve's behalf if he had a 10.4 ERA and couldn't get anybody out?' The answer is yes and that is why I'm here. It was a pretty tough day. First-year manager. Stick was alright. Jack was cool as a cucumber. He had been through quite a few wars before. I just kind of followed their lead."

And then they returned to the park where many in the crowd did not know anything was amiss.

"I didn't get back until the third or fourth inning and we were behind 6-0 when we got back. I can remember putting on my uniform in my office. Stick was in there and I was thinking, 'the way this game is going, maybe I should just stay in here'. But I get out and I believe it goes, 6-1, 7-2, 7-3, 7-5, 8-5, 8-6, 8-7. I remember Pat Kelly got a basehit and we won the game 9-8."

Bleeding Pinstripe

Buck Showalter summarizes his time in the Yankee organization as follows:

"It was home, still is. It was an honor. I was a Yankee 19 years. I still consider myself a Yankee. It was where I was raised in baseball. There is a majority of my heart that will always be there."

Exiting Stage Right

In the wake of the Yankees' first playoff appearance in 14 years, suddenly, Buck Showalter was gone.

"I knew that under the circumstances Mr. Steinbrenner offered me the contract there was no way I could have done the job that needed to be done there with coaches that weren't mine. There wasn't anything else to it. If I could have kept my coaches, I would have stayed there until they ran me out of there. I left and didn't have a thing to stand on. I remember telling Angela, 'We may be in A-ball next year, who knows what's gonna happen. But I can't turn my back on these guys.' I couldn't watch him put coaches in that locker room that weren't mine. Everybody since then has been able to do that. I think he understands how important that is now."

Regrets?

Since Buck Showalter exited the organization, the Yankees came within three outs of winning four consecutive World Series.

"I don't think it's gut-wrenching to watch them. I think Joe realizes that there was quite a foundation that Gene Michael and a lot of people put together and he's kind of been a caretaker of it. I have a great deal of pride in what they've done. I know what it takes and what you have to do have championship clubs. To have all of that verified is very satisfying. I'm pulling for them. It's the first score I look for."

Buck Nostradamus

Know of anybody else in baseball history who helped craft the two teams that met each other in the World Series?

"Before the season started last year, ESPN asked all the baseball analysts to make predictions about divisional winners and go right on out. I picked Arizona and New York in the World Series with Arizona winning in seven games. They thought I was some kind of guru. But one guy said, 'Who else is he gonna pick?'"

Starting Small, I Mean, Real Small

I first interviewed Buck Showalter in 1986 when he managed the Oneonta Yankees of the New York-Penn League. He cherishes the experience.

"I was there in '85 and '86. Those years, I had spring training, ran extended spring in some place in the swamps of Florida. Then I went to Oneonta and then I headed right to the Instructional League. Angela and I went at it from February until November. You find out in a hurry if you want to do that for a living."

Even Then He Knew

Buck Showalter estimates that three-fourths of the players he had in extended spring training were first-year Latins.

"Bernie Williams, Hensley Meulens, Oscar Azocar, Deion Sanders was in extended spring."

Showalter had to talk Bernie Williams out of going home.

"He was so homesick. He wanted to quit switch-hitting. He was a 17-year-old kid who looked like Bambi drinking water out of a creek with the leaves rustling behind him. Beautiful man, though."

Just Back the Truck in on Payday, Won't Ya?

As Buck Showalter says, you find out in a hurry if you want to be in baseball.

"I was making twelve-five. I got a little stipend for the Instructional League. I went from $12,500 to $16,000 in '86. Then I got a three-year contract and thought I had the world by the coattails for 19, 25 and 32.

"Bobby Hoffman called me and asked me if I would consider signing a three-year deal. What else could you ask for, getting paid working for the Yankees and managing a baseball team?"

Bucky Dent

Just Call Me Babe

So what was the biggest swing that Bucky Dent ever had in his life prior to October 2, 1978 in the seventh inning in Boston, Massachusetts?

"To tell you the truth, I hit a home run in the All-Star Game for Cal Ripken Sr. in Double-A. I think it was the All-Stars against Montgomery. I think I hit the home run in the top of the ninth inning.

"It was as surprising then as the one in Boston."

Something to Remember Me By

Imagine what the life of Russell Earl Dent would be like if he never hammered that up-and-in fastball from Mike Torrez into the net above the Green Monster one late fall afternoon.

"The only thing it did was make me more visible. It was a big game that people remember and they remember me for it. As far as my life changing, I don't think anything would have changed except that people remember who I am and where they were when it happened."

Has it ever been a burden?

"No, never. It's been a lot of fun because you meet a lot of different people who talk about it all the time and

Bucky Dent

how it changed their lives. People talk about driving off the road. It's fun talking to those people because they can remember where they were and what they were doing at that time."

And it's a real goof every time he's in New England.

"Oh yeah, it is."

You have a new middle initial.

"Oh yeah," he said laughing. "F."

Don Zimmer

How Much is That Little Doggie in the Window?

Don Zimmer came to the major leagues with the Brooklyn Dodgers and played with pitcher Billy Loes, who once claimed that he lost a groundball in the sun.

"We were in Cincinnati and it was very close to the All-Star break. Buzzy Bavasi, the general manager, was on the trip with us. I might be wrong in numbers, but Billy was something like 10-1 or 12-1 or something. It was getaway day and Billy was walking down 5th and Vine and went by this little pet shop. He saw this puppy he liked. He went in and asked how much. Well, he didn't have that kind of money on him. He wanted to take the dog with him, put him on a plane and take him back with us to Brooklyn. So he went to Buzzy and asked if he could lend him two or three hundred dollars. And Buzzy said, 'For what?' Billy said, 'I saw a little puppy I wanted to buy and take home.'

"Buzzy said, 'I ain't giving you two or three hundred dollars to pay for some puppy to take back on the plane.'"

Here, Billy Loes took a stance.

"He says, 'If you don't wanna give me money to buy the dog, then the heck with it, I'm not pitching anymore.' Somebody said to him that he had a chance of winning 20 games. He said, 'What's the difference, if you win 20 games, then they're gonna expect you to do it every year.'"

The Zimmer Fence Company

A check-swing off the bat of Chuck Knoblauch in the postseason at Yankee Stadium struck Don Zimmer in the head, injuring his ear and eliciting the now-famous line, "100,000 ears in the ballpark and he had to get mine." Immediately thereafter, fences were erected in front of both dugouts, but they were not identical. On the fence in front of the Yankee dugout was a tiny white sign that reads: Zimmer Fence Company.

Here's the founder.

"When that ball hit me I thought I was hurt. I was stunned but not exactly knocked unconscious. But I went down. And when I went down I put my hand up to the left side of my head which I where I suffered a serious injury years ago. That's the first thing that came to my mind. I was numb. As I put my hand up, my hand's full of blood. I say, 'Oh my God, now what?' I'm laying there and they finally got me up and I can't believe how much blood I have in my hand."

At that time, Zim really didn't know exactly where he was hit.

"I was half foggy. They picked me up and laid me down up in the clubhouse and the doctor walked in. The first thing he said was, 'You're not even gonna need stitches.'

Don Zimmer and Joe Torre

That was kind a relief because, evidently, I wasn't cut that bad. What had happened after I was up on that table for a while and the doctors were looking at me and so forth was that I realized where I was hit. The ball hit me kind of in my neck underneath the jaw bone. It then went up and nicked my ear, sort of like the way you nick yourself shaving and the bleeding doesn't stop.

"That's where all the blood was coming from. I was relieved that it didn't me in my skull where I had been hurt before."

Enter The Boss.

"While I was in the trainers room and the trainers and doctors were looking at me, George Steinbrenner came in and said, 'Well, we're gonna have to do something out there to protect everyone more. We're gonna have to put up some kind of a fence or something.' That's where it started."

But that doesn't explain the lovely parting gifts, though.

"The next day, there was this box in my locker. I didn't know what it was. It was this old helmet. It looked like it had been in a war. I blamed Mel Stottlemyre, the prankster. I said, 'You do this, Mel?' He said, 'No.' Then I thought it was Jeter. I went out into the clubhouse and I said, 'You do this?' He said, 'No.' The only guy left I thought did this was Steinbrenner. I put the helmet on and he was in the clubhouse. I said, 'George, did you put this helmet on my chair?' He said, 'No I didn't put that helmet on your chair. You don't have guts enough to wear that in the dugout.' I never dreamt of ever wearing that helmet in the dugout until he said that."

That was good enough for Zim.

"I took the helmet and set it between Joe and I. We had to get up for the national anthem. When it was over, as the team took the field, I just let the helmet sit. When we came in off the field, I called Knoblauch over and said,

'Knobby, you have any objections about me wearing this helmet while you're hitting?' He said, 'No, I think it would be neat.' I wore the helmet for three pitches and that was it."

Somebody, though, took a picture and that picture remains in our mind's eye.

It's a Small World

One swing from Bucky Dent broke countless hearts in New England on October 2, 1978, including Don Zimmer's, the manager of the Red Sox that fateful day. Of course it would follow that Zimmer would come to the Yankees and wind up renting Dent's house in New Jersey.

"I was trying to find a nice place to live. At that time, most of the Yankee families lived over in Jersey. Well, I didn't even know where to start. I don't remember who said to me that Bucky Dent was trying to rent his house in Wyckoff. Somehow, my wife got a hold of somebody, I guess, another wife, and found Dent. That's how it happened. It was a very nice house."

The Bride Wore White . . . And Had Dust on Her Shoes

In 1951, Don Zimmer, playing for the Brooklyn Dodgers' farm club in Elmira, New York, got married at home plate.

"We had a general manager by the name of Spencer Harris. He had been with the Dodgers for years. He had been down in Fort Worth as a general manager before that.

He heard Ed Roebuck, who was a pitcher, and I in club-house talking about getting married. And when he heard that, his eyes perked up. He said, 'Would the two of you be interested in getting married at home plate?'

Presumably, Zimmer and Roebuck were not getting married to each other.

"He said he had a couple of weddings like that in Fort Worth. We both kind of shook our heads. We thought that would be kind of neat. But it turned out when Eddie went home, either his family or her family didn't like the idea of getting married at home plate. They thought they ought to get married in church. He wound up backing out. So my wife and I went on and got married at home plate." *That Night!*

"Eddie and Janice got married that afternoon. Roebuck, being a starting pitcher, got to go on a three-day honeymoon. I played that night."

15 minutes later.

9
FRONT OFFICE

Clyde King

DH, You're the One

In 2002, Clyde King begins his 27th year in the Yankee organization. How many people can boast of that?

"I wish everybody knew George Steinbrenner like I know him. His compassion for people that work for him."

You're kidding?

"No. He's tough sometimes, but he's never really mean to you. He may say something that appears to be mean at the time but he'll come back later and make things better. He's just been a wonderful person to work for. It hasn't always been easy working for him but it hasn't always been difficult working for him, either. I would say the majority of the time it has been absolutely fabulous. You know, as you go through the valley with George Steinbrenner, the valley is not very deep. You don't stay in it very long. You're back on the mountaintop soon. The thing about Mr. Steinbrenner is he never expects any of us to do anything he wouldn't do. I never had a problem putting in hours for him."

One Score Ago

In 1982, George Steinbrenner asked Clyde King, who managed Atlanta and San Francisco previously, to leave the front office and replace Gene Michael as manager. This was one of those schizophrenic years. Michael had replaced Bob Lemon.

"I really was not gung-ho managing. I didn't want to manage that year where the players were difficult to discipline. Mr. Steinbrenner is a disciplinarian, just like I am. I think that's one reason we got along. I wanted players to be on time and if they messed up, I wanted to be able to fine them. At that time, you couldn't fine a player more than $500 without going to arbitration, terrible things like that."

King enjoyed the work he was doing upstairs.

"I was doing advance scouting ahead of the team, looking at players we were interested in. When I went back down there, though, I enjoyed it. Several people said I changed the attitude of the team. We had a lot of guys hurt. That was the reason it was going poorly for Gene Michael. We just weren't up to par."

Clyde King won 29 games and lost 33 as Yankee manager. The club finished fifth, 79-83, 16 games behind division-leading Milwaukee.

Bob Watson

All Screwed Up

Bob Watson says, "It wasn't too much fun sometimes as the GM. It was another story when I played for the Yankees in 1980.

"We were at the Stadium playing Detroit in a doubleheader the final Saturday of the season. We won the first game and clinched the division pennant. So a lot of the regulars were given the second game off."

Manager Dick Howser started Bobby Brown in center. The switch-hitter was facing lefthander John Hiller.

"Hiller's best pitch was a change-up. Bobby Brown was a better hitter from the left side but he had to bat righthanded which he was not that good at but he was very strong on the right side. Brown leads off the game and I think Hiller jumps out in front of him like 1 and 2."

He throws him a change-up.

"Bobby starts his swing and sees that it is a change-up. He stops his swing but he stops it so hard and so abrupt that he hits himself in the head with the bat and goes down to his knees. Everybody in the dugout is just rolling. He looks over into the dugout and barely sees Howser and Yogi because everyone is laying on the floor in the dugout just laughing."

They say imitation is the sincerest form of flattery.

"For the remainder of the game, somebody says, 'Instant replay' and they would grab a bat, check their swing, hit themselves in the head and fall down to their knees. The game is over, we had just clinched the pennant and instead of a wild celebration, they were doing this Bobby Brown thing. It was one of the funniest things I remember seeing with the Yankees or anywhere else."

Setting the Record Straight

The popular notion in New York is that Bob Watson left as General Manager of the Yankees, the first African-American in baseball history to hold that position, to save his life, that working for George Steinbrenner was killing him.

"George Steinbrenner didn't help my health situation but he didn't cause it. I had it when I came. I had high blood pressure basically all my life. It runs in my family. What I did with the Yankees I did with Houston. I put in a lot of hours. I was trying to prove something not only to myself but to the baseball world that minorities have what it takes to run a ballclub. George had very little to do with me running myself into a health situation that I definitely had to leave. But he didn't cause it."

10
BROADCASTERS

Bill White

The Call of the Home Run of Russell Earl Dent

We hear it every year, Bill White's play-by-play call of Bucky Dent's cataclysmic playoff home run in 1978. Listen closely and he sounds surprised as the ball disappears over the Green Monster.

"Well, you don't know. You can't be surprised by anything up there. The fence is short and if you get under the ball, it's a home run. So it wasn't a surprise. Rizzuto taught me how to sound surprised."

Sending a Message

When the Yankees cast the net for a new broadcaster, Michael Burke was on a mission. Bill White said the club president wanted the ballclub to reflect the community.

"Mike Burke said he wanted a black broadcaster. He said, 'We're in the Bronx. We've got a lot of Hispanic people here. We have a lot of black people here and I want these young kids to realize they can do this.' With Mike, I think it was a social statement to the minority people in New York. To me, it was a challenge."

Especially when a front office official named Howard Berk called him.

"Somebody sent him a letter and had cancelled their box seats. It didn't disturb me but surprised me that somebody who could afford to buy box seats and obviously should be well-to-do was disturbed simply because a black man was going to broadcast Yankee baseball."

Later on, White asked Berk what happened.

"The guy must have had some clout because he got the tickets back, which disturbed me. I thought that if he felt that way, they shouldn't have given him the tickets back. They should have sold them to somebody else. In fact, I would have bought them if I had known that he wanted them back."

Scooter Scoots

It was the ninth inning of a Yankees nighttime exhibition game in Fort Lauderdale when Phil Rizzuto asked Frank Messer if he could get him anything. Messer made the huge mistake of asking for coffee. With that, Rizzuto exited.

Bill White had left the park in the sixth inning to pick up his daughters at the airport.

"When I got back to the hotel, the game was in the 17th inning about one or two o'clock in the morning and I heard Frank Messer doing the ballgame."

The next morning, White is back at the park preparing for another game. In pops Rizzuto and says the following: "Hey, Frank, here's that cup of coffee you wanted."

With Rizzuto, no two days were ever the same because no one ever knew what would come out of that mouth.

"We could rip each other a little bit. He'd call me 'a National Leaguer' and I'd call him 'a little bunter'. We never had, in my opinion, a cross word with each other. We never, over the 18 years I worked with him, had any kind of animosity."

Joe Garagiola

The Best Fiction Writer Couldn't Make This Up

Little Joe Garagiola and little Lawrence Peter Berra were best friends growing in an Italian neighborhood in St. Louis known as 'The Hill.'

So imagine the emotions stirring inside Joe G when he broadcast the 1964 World Series for NBC which pitted the St. Louis Cardinals against Yogi's Yankees.

"It was one of those moments if I would have dwelled upon it a little bit, I would have gotten goosebumps from it. He got fired right after that and lost it, I think, with the tying run at second base. We both thought he was gonna get rehired with a long-term contract."

Berra was gone to the Mets as a player/coach, just missing the collapse, as Garagiola was hired by the Yankees.

"That would have been neat but it was not to be. I was kind of glad because that was not a good team to manage."

Welcome to New York

After the 1964 World Series, Yogi Berra was not the only legend exiting the organization under bizarre circumstances. So did Mel Allen, replaced by Joe Garagiola.

"I was doing Game of the Week. A guy who was in charge of broadcasting for the club was the same guy I had worked for at NBC.

"Ralph Houk, who was now general manager, called me and asked if I would be interested in the Yankee job. I said, 'Absolutely. You'd be crazy not to be interested in it.' So he offered it to me and the next thing you know, I was broadcasting for the Yankees. I made it a point to say that there's no way you replace Mel Allen. He was perfect for the Yankees with that voice of his. He was just a tradition. For me to broadcast Yankee games it was great. There it was, Yankee Stadium, and I was working with Rizzuto, Jerry Coleman and Red Barber."

John Gordon

Sticking Up For a Guy

John Gordon had long held aspirations to broadcast major league baseball. He thought he had made it, then he didn't, then he did.

"I became very good friends with Gene Michael. He managed the Columbus Clippers in '79. It's ironic. I was out of baseball in 1981. I had been with the Clippers from 1977 through 1980. Just through circumstances, I took a TV job in Columbus and had kind of decided I wasn't gonna get to the big leagues so I pursued this television opportunity."

That year, Gordon was calling the Liberty Bowl between Ohio State and Navy in Memphis.

"On our way, I got a call from a guy in New York and I had no idea who he was. He said there was an opening in the Yankee booth and asked if I would be interested. I called Stick and he wanted to know what they were offering. I went up to New York and they made me an offer. When I went back to Columbus, I called Stick and said they offered three years and good money. At the time I questioned working for Steinbrenner, an issue, if not the most important issue. Stick said, 'Hey, they offered you a three-year deal. If it doesn't work out, it's three years you can write off as an experience.' So we accepted the position and were off and running in 1982."

John Gordon spent five seasons with the Yankees through 1986. He walked into a World Championship with the Minnesota Twins in 1987, with whom he remains, uncontracted, in 2002.

You-Know-Who Was on the Bridge
Scooter Scoots

"We had a game that went 17 innings. Scooter left like in the ninth like he always would. We struggled in the 15th, 16th and 17th innings. There were 2,000 people left in the stands. We were just trying to get through the ballgame. Steinbrenner was listening. It was one of the very few times that he ever really meddled. Usually, when the ballclub was going bad, that was when we had our best broadcasts because he never meddled. When the ballclub was going good, that was when we had our toughest broadcasts because he would get involved. In this instance, Frank Messer and I were on the air and Scooter was gone.

"It was tough. Steinbrenner called the broadcast director and wanted to know where Scooter was. He had crossed the bridge."

Hey, Scooter, this one is for you.

"The very next week we had another 17-inning game. Scooter stuck around. He didn't leave because the hammer had come down. We were doing the 17th inning like it was the seventh game of the World Series. You never heard a more exciting broadcast."